The L.A. Musical History TOUR

Second Edition

A Guide to the Rock and Roll Landmarks of Los Angeles

2.13.61

P.O. BOX 1910 · LOS ANGELES ·
CALIFORNIA · 90078 · USA

The L.A. Rock and Roll History Tour (second edition)
©1998 Art Fein

Published in the United States by 2.13.61 Publications, P.O. Box 1910, Los Angeles, CA 90078.

Additional writers:

Frank Zappa former residence (Laurel Canyon) text by Mark Leviton

Chadney's, Dionysus Records, Jelly Roll Morton, Johnny "Guitar" Watson and Frank Zappa former residence (Los Angeles) by Skip Heller

Electro-Vox, Sound City, Studio 56 and TTG text by Rob Santos

Design: **ENDLESS** ∞
Cover Design: Chapple Design

To my mother, who stuck by me through thick and thin—mostly thin.

I know of no one more qualified to write about the people and places of Los Angeles than my dear and longtime friend Art Fein. I think everyone will enjoy and find his book as interesting, educational and fascinating as I did.

—Phil Spector / Los Angeles, 1998

INTRODUCTION

After re-reading my original intro to the first edition of this book, I have to note some changes: L.A. is not the heavy-metal capital it was in 1991, and disco came back sort of. But what's most evident in retrospect is a change: in 1991 I was a fire-breathing zealot hammering home the message of L.A.'s pivotal and overlooked place in the development of rock & roll — I'm even more fanatical now.

You wanna use the word "organic" when you talk about southern California? Well don't talk about bean sprouts or pesticide-free fruit — talk about the natural emergence of rock & roll here in its birthplace.

There is a famous photo of black musician Big Jay McNeely lying on the stage of the Olympic Auditorium in October 1951, blowing his sax while white and Chicano admirers howl in ecstasy.* Without any leaders, kids in L.A. freely and naturally engaged in mixed-race appreciation of R&B, which flourished here alongside jazz. (It has been posited by historians Jim Dawson and Steve Propes** that Illinois Jacquet's honking-sax solo in an all-star jazz jam at L.A.'s Philharmonic Hall in 1944 was the opening blast of rock & roll. Once you hear it, on the cut "Blues" on the album *Jazz At The Philharmonic*, you, too, may be swayed.) Then as today, L.A. was the melting pot. Racially-mixed music formed here then became "rock & roll."

I must adjust the previous Intro's dismissal of L.A. as a generator of country music. As is well known, California was the destination of Dust Bowl and other settlers during the Great Depression. The settlers planted their music and nurtured it. Okie emigrants The Maddox Brothers and Rose relocated here from Fresno in a migratory pattern that became familiar - Alabama's Merle Travis settled here, Tennessee Ernie Ford came too, Jimmy Wakely came along with thousands and thousands of other immigrants. Country music flourished on tv here in the mid-1950s with many regular country music shows, incuding Cliffie Stone's "Hometown Jamboree", Tex Ritter's "Barn Dance" and "Cal's Corral." That many had a "western" orientation is not surprising. "Western" music abounded, not only in movies with the thousands of genuine cowboys working here in industry, agriculture — and movies.

L.A. is still America's, and the world's, cultural whipping boy, and that bias infects the perception of our rock & roll significance. The Rock & Roll Hall Of Fame, founded in part by a San Francisco-originated magazine noted for dishing Zappa, The Doors, and most things L.A. in the late 1960s and 1970s, has not yet deigned to designate L.A. as a power-base in rock & roll history, though it has afforded a space to—surprise!—Frisco. Tsk tsk. And recently an English bloke wrote a cynical book about L.A.'s rock & roll history that was hailed by the ignorami as spot-on. In truth (a quality scattershot through his tome) it stained only the writer, not the city.

Do we care? Not a dead medfly. We're here, and we're rich every day for it. Let's all join hands and shout "L.A. is the rock & roll center of the world!"

—Art Fein
Los Angeles, 1998

*When that photo was taken Alan Freed was still a classical music deejay in Cleveland.
**In their book *What Was The First Rock & Roll Record* (Faber & Faber, 1993).

A&M RECORDS
1416 N. La Brea
Hollywood

Though the record company itself has made history during its thirty-year run, the very ground on which A&M stands is historic. Its location is in the studio that Charlie Chaplin built in 1918 and the lot on which "Superman" and "Perry Mason" were filmed. But maybe in the final analysis this location will be remembered more as the place that spawned Herb

Alpert's Tijuana Brass, The Carpenters, Joe Cocker, Supertramp, Sting, Sheryl Crow, Blues Traveler and Chris Cornell (it is also where "We Are the World" was recorded) more than as a piece of film and television history. Starting their label in a garage studio, A&M founders Herb Alpert and Jerry Moss built their enterprise into one that spanned the globe and still does (though now under the aegis of PolyGram, since its sale to the Dutch media giant in 1990).

ACADEMY OF NUDE WRESTLING
(former location)
7736 Santa Monica Blvd.
West Hollywood

In the specially boxed 1974 Alice Cooper *Muscle of Love* album, the band is pictured in sailor suits in front of a mocked-up "Institute of Nude Wrestling," which was modeled on a real place. The year was 1973, *Deep Throat* was big news, and the area surrounding its showcase, The Pussycat Theater, rose to the occasion and sprouted allied businesses, including The Academy of Nude Wrestling. No one who went in there will now admit to it, so certain questions remain unanswered: Did the patron wrestle the live nude girl literally or philosophically? Was the Marquis of Queensberry respected? Did the Academy issue a diploma? No matter—the place lasted about a year, then vanished without a trace, but by inspiring the Alice Cooper album art it earned a place in rock history.

THE ACTION
(former location)
8265 Santa Monica Blvd.
West Los Angeles

A Hollywood hot-spot during the big music explosion of 1964, this place was frequented by movie and rock stars. Photographer Julian Wasser took a series of photos of Brian Jones dancing here, and another photographer, Henry Diltz, played here many times with his

band the Modern Folk Quartet. Diltz also remembers Frank Zappa hanging around outside the club a lot. That figures, The Mothers Of Invention made their debut here in early 1966 and were signed on the spot by producer Tom Wilson. The club changed to The Chez in late 1966 and is now a drycleaners.

AL'S BAR
305 South Hewitt
Downtown Los Angeles

The little door with the porthole is the entryway to the long enduring Al's Bar, the central music locus of the downtown art crowd. Here, adjacent to the artist-filled American Hotel, proprietor Mark Reisel has presented a broad cross section of L.A. music, ranging from Ry Cooder to Mojo Nixon to Fear, for more than ten years. Most recently artists such as The Mentors (played their last show here), Beck and Dwight Yoakam have played at Al's. Kind of like The Cavern in Liverpool, the place is dank and dark but "colorful." This area, a bit east of downtown's Little Tokyo, is still artist loft ridden and industrial, so Al's will probably stay agreeably funky for the foreseeable future—at least until property values rise.

ALCO RESEARCH & ENGINEERING
(former location)
6201 Santa Monica Blvd.
Hollywood

Alco, founded by Les Cottrell and Al Levine, pressed records for big West Coast labels including Alladin, Dore, Era, and Specialty (and for smaller labels such as Candix and X, which produced the first Beach Boys' record) through the late 1970s. In addition, their in-house labels included Lute ("Alley Oop") and 4J ("My Wife Can't Cook" by Lonnie Russ). In the 1980s this building was the home of Macola Records.

ALEXANDRIA HOTEL
5th & Spring
Downtown Los Angeles

Once a glorious hostel for kings and nabobs, this place had tumbled pretty far down when in 1985 it hosted a bunch of concerts. Calling their club Charley's Obsession, they presented Husker Du, Tom Tom Club, Specimen, and several other hot current bands in the hotel's ballroom. Like many of the floating clubs of the early to mid-eighties, it made its mark and then vanished. Dwight Yoakam's "Little Sister" video was filmed here.

LEE ALLEN CRYPT
(unmarked)
Inglewood Memorial Park

Lee Allen was THE rock & roll sax player but he wasn't much noticed on his own (he had a hit record "Walking With Mr. Leo" in 1958) , he played on most of Fats Domino's and Little Richard's hits. In demand until his death in 1995, Allen was an official member of The Blasters in the 1980s when he wasn't doing sessions or traveling with Fats. His trek from Pittsburgh, Kansas (his birthplace) to Denver (college) to New Orleans (where he arrived for rock & roll's birth) to L.A. was one triumphant journey.

ALLIGATOR LOUNGE
(former location)
3321 Pico Blvd.
Santa Monica

Throughout most of the 1990s this rootsabilly, blues, World Music, rock & roll club was a venerable and valuable part of the musical landscape presenting Big Sandy, Dave Alvin, Rose Maddox, Rosie Flores, Flaco Jiminez and Harvey Sid Fisher, among others. Closed in '97.

ALTA-CIENEGA MOTEL
1005 N. La Cienega
West Hollywood

Jim Morrison would often sleep off his binges at this place across the street from—and therefore convenient to—The Doors' business office at 8512 Santa Monica.

AMERICAN MUSIC PUBLISHING
(former location)
9109 Sunset Blvd.
Beverly Hills

Musician/publisher/manager Jerry Capehart issued records on the Crest, Silver, and Capehart labels in the 1950s and 1960s from this location. He had a couple of hits with "Turn Around, Look At Me" by Glen Campbell and "You're The Reason" by Bobby Edwards, but he is probably best known for managing and producing Eddie Cochran (whose first solo record "Skinny Jim" was a flop on Crest). Capehart got Cochran signed to Liberty, where he was a hit-making machine until his tragic death in a car crash in England in 1960 (See EDDIE COCHRAN GRAVE).

AMERICAN RECORDING
(former locations)
6229 Sunset Blvd. (1958-1962)
11386 Ventura, Studio City (1962-1982)

Founded by Mike and Ethel Podolor in 1958, this studio's first location, adjacent to the Hollywood Palladium, was the recording site of "Alley Oop," "A Thousand Stars," "Please Mr. Custer," and "Teen Beat." In the late 60s, after the studio had relocated to Studio City, the Podolor's son Richie and partner Bill Cooper recorded The Standells, Chocolate Watchband, Steppenwolf, Three Dog Night, Blues Image and many other hit acts. American is still active in Woodland Hills.

ANTELOPE VALLEY FAIRGROUNDS
Exposition Hall
Lancaster

This was the site of Captain Beefheart's first live performance. Beefheart (Don Van Vliet) became an alternative music icon before there was such a thing with his blues-growling and deceptively titled debut album *Safe As Milk*. He was at first associated with his former Antelope Valley high school classmate Frank Zappa.

THE ANTI-CLUB
4658 Melrose Ave.
Hollywood

A good place for bands on their way up, the Anti-Club has stood its ground for more than a decade as a showcase for every kind of rock. Among the bands that have played here are Black Flag, Chris Isaak, and Dwight Yoakam. There have also been art shows and the occasional poetry reading. Owner Helen and booker Reine Rivers provide the rock community with a much needed outlet for its energy.

THE AQUARIUS THEATER
6230 Sunset Blvd.
Hollywood

This Hollywood landmark, across the street from the Hollywood Palladium, has had many faces. Opened in 1938 as Earl Carroll's Vanities, it presented top musicians and "Hollywood's Most Beautiful Girls." In the 1950s it was the Moulin Rouge, featuring popular show business acts like Louis Prima and Keely Smith with Sam Butera and the Witnesses. Early in 1965 it was the site of the A.I.P. concert movie *The Big T.N.T. Show*, a follow up to 1964 T.A.M.I. Show (See SANTA MONICA CIVIC AUDITORIUM), featuring Ike and Tina Turner, The Byrds, Bo Diddley, The Ronettes, and many others, backed by an orchestra led by Phil Spector. The local scene swelled here too, with homegrowns (Seeds, Palace Guard, Merry-Go-Round, Electric Prunes), and a rash of San Jose transplants (Count V, Syndicate of Sound, Chocolate Watchband). On December 9, 1965 the building was renamed Hullabaloo (it was run by L.A. deejay Dave Hull—no connection to the hit TV show). Jan and Dean, Chad and Jeremy, Gary Lewis and The Playboys, The Turtles, and The Yardbirds were some of the acts that played this teen-oriented club during the mid-sixties. When music turned psychedelic, the site followed suit and on March 22, 1968, Kaleidoscope debuted. This club had floated from It's Boss (See CIRO'S) to the Cocoanut Grove (See COCOANUT GROVE) before landing here, presenting "Fillmore"-style acts like Jefferson Airplane, The Doors, Big Brother and The Holding Company, Canned Heat, The Youngbloods, Bo Diddley, and Fever Tree. That scene waned and the theater, renamed The Aquarius, entered the seventies with the long-running musical play, Hair and in 1974 presented the stage version of Tommy, starring Teddy Neely. It also has a television past. In the early 1950s it was the site of "Queen for a Day," and more recently for "Star Search" and other TV productions. It was briefly notorious as The Chevy Chase Theater, and in 1998 was occupied by Nickelodeon.

ART FEIN MOMENT #1
Argyle On-Ramp to 101
Freeway
Hollywood

In early 1973, your author picked up a bearded hitchhiker here and drove him to North Hollywood. Seeing record company material in the car the hitcher said "I've made a couple of records." I nodded, and then he said, "Yeah, I've got a couple of gold records at home." When I asked his name, he said "Sam Samudio." This is where I picked up Sam The Sham hitchhiking.

THE ASH GROVE

(former location)
8162 Melrose Ave.
Hollywood

The folk/blues club of the 1960's—John Lee Hooker, Bonnie Raitt, Muddy Waters, Lightnin' Hopkins, Sonny Terry, Brownie McGhee, Clifton Chenier and T-Bone Walker played here. Dig the diversity of this booking over a few months in 1964: Bill Monroe & His Bluegrass Boys, John Coltrane, John Lee Hooker, Ravi Shankar. After the last of many fires, The Ash Grove closed in November 1973, and the Improv moved in, rebuilding the interior to house a comedy club that has prospered ever since. The Ash Grove's closing left a great gap in the local music scene.

THE ASH GROVE

(former location)
250 Santa Monica Pier
Santa Monica

Risen at last from the ashes of the original Ash Grove, owner Ed Pearl opened this new attractive club in 1995. It closed in 1997.

ASSOCIATION HOUSE

65 N. Ardmore
Hollywood
(Do Not Disturb Occupants)

In the heady first days of folk rock circa 1965, most members of The Association (then in residence at the Troubadour as The Men, wearing billowy shirts and manly britches) lived at this party house, visited by many people from the burgeoning L.A. scene including Van Dyke Parks, Donovan, Ruthann Friedman (she composed "Windy"), Kim Fowley, a Smothers sister (!), and others.

THE ATOMIC CAFE

(former location)
422 East First St.
Los Angeles

In vogue in the early eighties when the punk scene flourished downtown, this diner didn't draw so much for its cuisine (you <u>have</u> lived if you've never tried their fried baloney chop suey) as for its name and ambiance: nondescript fifties decor, wall-to-wall mohawks and a great jukebox. A couple of doors down was the floating punk club The Brave Dog. The 1982 film *Atomic Cafe* must have drawn some inspiration from this place as they were both popular the same year. The Plugz song "Adolescent," cites "Hanging out at the Atomic Cafe" and The Motels do "Atomic Cafe" on their first album. In the spring of 1990 the old *Atomic Cafe* lettering was scraped from the window and the building was remodeled. It now houses a restaurant called Señor Fish.

BARNEY'S BEANERY

8447 Santa Monica Blvd.
West Hollywood

Did Janis Joplin really hit Jim Morrison with a Southern Comfort bottle here? It's easy to imagine, since they both hung out at Barney's in the late 1960s (she partied here and at The Troubadour the night she died). Barney's has long been home to rockers, actors and bikers on all rungs of the social ladder. Its three rooms house pool tables, booths, and a bar in a smokey truck-stop-like atmosphere that is earthy and real—an oddity in Hollywood. (But it's more genteel than in the past—fairly recently they removed their "No Faggots Allowed" sign from the bar.) Barney's offers forty chili dishes, 140 hamburger arrangements and claim to carry 293 kinds of beer. It ain't your California haute cuisine.

BARRIS KUSTOM AUTO

10811 Riverside Dr.
North Hollywood

In business customizing hot rods long before the advent of rock and roll, George "Kustom King" Barris still holds forth from this Valley site, modifying machinery for the movie and music industries. Barris is the man who modified two famous cars for James Dean: the mercury he drove in *Rebel Without a Cause* and the Porsche Spyder he drove to his death. His

list of custom vehicle customers is awesome: Elvis Presley (whose Barris-Kustomed gold-flecked Cadillac is now at the Country Music Hall of Fame in Nashville), James Brown, Roy Orbison, David Lee Roth, Prince (Purple Rain motorcycle), Bobby Darin, Trini Lopez and he did a psychedelic paint job on John Lennon's Rolls Royce. The list is endless, and the showroom fascinating, both for the custom machines on hand and the wall photos of movie, TV and rock stars and their cars. In 1997, rumors spread that Barris was closing because they were shipping their famous cars to the Star Car Museum in Gatlinsburg, Tennessee, however, Barris remains—duplicates were sent to Tennessee.

BEATLES RESIDENCE 1964
356 St. Pierre Road
Bel Air
(Do Not Disturb Occupants)

The Beatles had booked a suite of rooms at the Ambassador Hotel for their August 23, 1964 appearance at the Hollywood Bowl, but as the threat of thousands of teenage Beatlemaniacs trampling their grounds grew real, the hotel canceled the group's reservations. This house, the home of British actor Reginald Owen, was commandeered (well, rented for four days for $1,000) and renamed Beatle Manor. Upon entering the house, John Lennon headed directly to the pool and jumped in fully clothed.

BEATLES RESIDENCE, 1965
2850 Benedict Canyon
Bel Air
(Do Not Disturb Occupants)

When the Beatles came back to L.A. on August 23, 1965 for their August 29th & 30th Hollywood Bowl shows, they were billeted at this mountainside dwelling far from the madding crowd—but some stealthy fans set up camp in the driveway and some more enterprising ones hired a helicopter to circle the place so they could gaze down on their idols. (The house's next residents were Herman's Hermits, who stayed here while making the unforgettable—to them—feature film *Hold On*, not be confused with the Sam and Dave song "Hold On, I'm Coming," which the Hermits would never do.)

BEATLES RESIDENCE, 1966
7655 Curson Terrace
Hollywood
(Do Not Disturb Occupants)

When the Beatles were in town on August 24, 1966, for their last L.A. appearance at Dodger Stadium, their holing up here was not a well-kept secret. Police barricades where set up at the bottom of Curson Avenue at Franklin and residents like "Shindig" host Jimmy O'Neill had to undergo stringent security screening before being allowed up their own street. (After 11:00 P.M. the police department maintained a full-time shuttlebus, taking young Beatle fans to a holding area where their parents could pick them up.) Beatles party guest Rodney Bingenheimer remembers fans crawling up the steep dirt mountainside to get a glimpse of the goings-on, and partygoers throwing steaks to (at?) them. In 1968, the Jefferson Airplane stayed at this same place when they were recording their *Crown of Creation* album.

THE BEL AIR CLUB
(former location)
312 Catalina
Redondo Beach

This is where surf music began. In 1961, The Belairs, a local beach band, played rock and roll instrumentals for the beach crowd. Their self-penned "Mr. Moto" became a local hit and for about a year they held sway here inspiring scores of imitators, among them the teenaged Beach Boys. This club—named after them, not the other way around—was their headquarters during the headspinning summer of 1962. (Simultaneously, Dick Dale was holding forth at the Rendezvous Ballroom in Balboa [See HARMONY PARK, RENDEZVOUS BALLROOM]). A couple of years later deejay Reb Foster renamed it The Rebellaire Club and held "Battle of the Bands" contests, which The Crossfires (who became The Turtles) won several times. Belairs guitarist Paul Johnson returned here in 1966 with a new and timely band, The Everpresent Fullness, when the place was renamed the Third i.

JESSE BELVIN GRAVE
Evergreen Memorial Park
204 N. Evergreen
Boyle Heights

Jesse Belvin was a talented singer, songwriter and arranger who had a tremendous influence on Los Angeles R&B. He sang with numerous groups in the early 1950s, coached and nurtured other singers and groups and co-wrote "Earth Angel" with Curtis Williams of The Penguins. His biggest solo recording, "Goodnight My Love," did not crack the pop charts in 1956 despite its status now as a classic oldie, but another ballad, "Guess Who," written by his wife Jo Anne, was a huge crossover hit in 1959. Both Belvin and his wife died in a car crash near Hope, Arkansas on February 6, 1960.

BEN FRANK'S
(former location)
8585 Sunset Blvd.
West Hollywood

This place had been standing since the fifties, with its proto-Googie's architecture and American cuisine. Its location and all-night hours made it a late-night hangout for musicians of all stripes: The Kinks, The Byrds, Little Richard, Lovin' Spoonful, Led Zeppelin, ad infinitum. In the song "Suzi Creemcheese," Frank Zappa says, "Let's ditch Canter's and go to Ben Frank's." This was in the mid-1960s when those restaurants were two of the few places that would serve longhairs. In 1966, when producers were casting "The Monkees" TV show (folk singer Stephen Stills auditioned, but was not chosen), their trade paper ads said they were seeking "Ben Frank's types." A year later, Byrds roadie Bryan MacLean, left behind when The Byrds toured Europe, was introduced to singer Arthur Lee in the Ben Frank's parking lot, and together they formed the group Love. A character on the Tom Waits album *Small Change* (1976) waits at Ben Frank's for "The One That Got Away." For years Ben Frank's remained a good place for after-hours rock-star rubber-necking and, of course, dining, until it closed in 1997. It is now a Mel's Drive in.

BENNY K'S
(former location)
Santa Monica & La Jolla
West L.A.

When this was a local pub in 1973, the house band, The Alligators, was the only band in L.A. playing rockabilly for a living (and not much of one). In 1996, band leader Dollar Varden issued his old band's tapes on a Garage Records CD which he called *Pre-X Zoom* owing to the fact that his lead was Billy Zoom in 1976. (Strictly speaking it oughta've been called Pre-Zoom Kendall, as Zoom was still known then by his previous name, Ty Kendall.)

RICHARD BERRY CRYPT
Inglewood Memorial Park

Richard Berry, the man who wrote "Louie Louie," and whom Frank Zappa called "one of the most important secret sources behind West Coast r&b in the 1950s," was interred here in 1995. (See LOUIE LOUIE BIRTHPLACE.)

BETWEEN CLARK AND HILLDALE
Sunset Strip

When Arthur Lee of Love (an intensely popular mid-sixties L.A. band who had national hits with "Little Red Book" and "7 and 7 Is") wrote this song he was referring to this strip which contained nightclubs and restaurants that comprised the center of the Sunset Strip. Left to right (then): Hamburger Hamlet (James Dean hung out there), The Galaxy (where Iron Butterfly was the house band and Edward James Olmos' band Eddie and the Tide played a lot. Later converted into Johnny Rivers' music publishing office), The London Fog (small club where The Doors played; formerly the folk-music Unicorn club; later Sneaky Pete's; now Duke's) and the Whisky-A-Go-Go.

THE BEVERLY HILLS HOTEL
9641 Sunset Blvd.
Beverly Hills

Many theories exist about what hotel is pictured on the cover of the Eagle's *Hotel California* album; looking at the Spanish towers, it resembles famous hotels in Santa Barbara and Riverside. But it was actually The Beverly Hills Hotel, shot from Sunset Boulevard. The reason you don't readily recognize it is that photographer David Alexander shot it from a fifty-foot fire department "cherrypicker." (The interior shot for the album was taken at the Lido Apartments. See LIDO.) In late 1967, Mike Nesmith had a showdown with Monkees creator Don Kirschner in his bungalow here demanding that the group be allowed to play on their own records or he would quit the band. He won, then he quit anyway. (Nesmith's "Different Drum" was a hit for Linda Ronstadt & The Stone Poneys while Nesmith was still a Monkee.) The Beverly Hills Hotel

is, of course, a noted hostelry for movie stars, rock stars, and people who like to be paged in the Polo Lounge. John Lennon and Yoko Ono used to stay in the back bungalows, separated from the main body of the hotel, during the early seventies.

BEVERLYWOOD SWIMMING SCHOOL
2612 S. Robertson
Los Angeles

Photographer Kirk Weddle shot the baby in the swimming pool for the cover of Nirvana's *Nevermind* in this pool. The band had initially been fascinated by a similar photo supplied by a photo service, but that photographer wanted too much money so Weddle supplied the excellent substitution instead. (The record company was initially reluctant to release the photo showing a baby penis, but sample opinions proved baby penises to not be as horrifying as grownup ones.)

BIDO LITO'S BACKSTAGE
(former location)
1608 Cosmo
Hollywood

Bido Lito's Backstage (it adjoins the Ivar Theater—See IVAR) was a popular rock and roll nightclub that was home base for Love and Iron Butterfly in 1966. In fact, Iron Butterfly lived upstairs of Bido Lito's for their first month in town after moving here from San Diego. (According to Rick Gagnon of Iron Butterfly, the song "Inagaddadavita" was written in an apartment above Bido Lito's and the song <u>was</u> called "In A Garden of Eden" before it got mangled.) Bido Lito's also featured The Seeds, The Doors, The Strawberry Alarm Clock and other local bands. Previously it was the folk-music club The Unicorn's second location, and Cosmo's Alley, a jazz/folk club where Lenny Bruce and Josh White appeared. (James Ellroy's novel *The Big Nowhere*, set in L.A. in 1950, refers to a Bido Lito's nightclub on South Central Avenue, leading one to think that such a club preceded this one in Hollywood. Not true: after checking with Ellroy, it turns out his Bido Lito's was a fictitious relocation.) During the seventies the club fell into anonymity but stayed put until the late 1980s when it reemerged as popular new night spot The Gaslight, featuring up-and-coming bands like Social Distortion, Haunted Garage, The Saddle Sores and Untamed Youth. In the mid 1990s it became The Opium Den and still plays host to an assortment of bands.

BILLBOARD LIVE

9039 Sunset Blvd.
West Hollywood

Built over the bones of Gazarri's (the club, not late owner Bill Gazarri), this hi-tech newcomer had a steady if unspectacular launch in 1996 featuring top-rated acts that can't or won't play the House of Blues. Now, as the Key Club, it is "4-walled," i.e., booked to different promoters every night.

MIKE BLOOMFIELD RESTING PLACE

Hillside Memorial Park
6001 W. Centinela
Culver City

Chicago-raised blues guitarist Mike Bloomfield made a big splash as part of the Paul Butterfield Blues Band, and then on Dylan's "Like A Rolling Stone" and the *Highway 61 Revisited* album, all in 1965. From there he helped form, and then quit, The Electric Flag, and remained one of the premiere guitarists of the 1960s, also playing on the big selling *Super-Session* album with Al Kooper and Stephen Stills, and on duet albums with Kooper. In the 70s his star waned and he made a living scoring porn films, all the while feeding a heroin habit that finally consumed him. A longtime Bay Area resident, Bloomfield was found dead of an overdose in his car in San Francisco in 1981.

BLUE JAY WAY

Sunset Strip hills

George Harrison rented a house on this street in 1968 just before the Beatles recorded *Magical Mystery Tour*. Their publicist Derek Taylor had such difficulty finding the place in the fog one night that Harrison penned a dreamy paean to it called "Blue Jay Way" which emerged on that album. The street might still be hard to find because residents report that the street sign is frequently stolen by Beatle(klepto)-maniacs.

BLUE SALOON
4657 Lankershim
North Hollywood

This once-innocuous neighborhood bar got red-hot in 1990 as THE showcase for the local roots-rock scene when Big Sandy & His Fly-Right Trio, The Dave & Deke Combo, Russell Scott & The Red Hots, Dee Lannon & The Rhythm Rustlers and Untamed Youth all held weekly slots and 50s idols like Sleepy Labeef and Rose Maddox played. But a rift with the club developed and one day, like the dinosaurs, these acts all disappeared. The club still is popular, booking local bands.

BOARDNERS
1652 Cherokee
Hollywood

An old-time "Hollywood" place (it still has old-style phone outlets in the booths for agents and big-shots), this watering-hole has a new tradition too, having been a musician hangout for more than ten years. In an office he rented above Boardners in the late 1970s, Stan Ridgeway wrote scores for porn films which eventually led to his forming Wall Of Voodoo.

THE BODY SHOP
8250 Sunset Blvd.
West Hollywood

In 1977 Warner Bros. Records presented Van Halen with their first gold record here in a ceremony hosted by Milton Berle, the uncle of their then-manager. In 1984 Mötley Crüe followed Van Halen's lead by receiving their gold record at the Kit Kat Club (now gone) on Santa Monica Blvd. Strip houses have long figured in L.A. rock history: The Roxy, Club 88 and The Ivar were all former strip palaces and Jim Morrison loved to go to the Phone Booth (See PHONE BOOTH).

BOMP RECORDS

(former location)
5230 Laurel Canyon
North Hollywood

Northern Californian Greg Shaw moved his 60s-focussed fanzine Who Put the Bomp to LA in the early 1970s when he was made editor of Phonograph Record Magazine, a feisty competitor for Rolling Stone which operated out of United Artists Records. In 1977 he and his wife Suzy opened a record store at this spot dedicated to punk-rock and other newly-emerging alternative forms of rock music. It held in-stores for many new up-and-coming bands including Blondie, Cheap Trick, and the Ramones, but the store, and the magazine, folded in 1978 when Shaw's newborn Bomp Records label began to consume all his time. Bomp Records issued many records by new bands and old, including Devo, The Shoes, The Romantics, 20/20, The Modern Lovers, The Germs, and Iggy Pop. (Peter Buck still has a tattered letter from Shaw rejecting an early R.E.M. demo.) Today Bomp has more than 400 albums in print, and a mail-order business run by ex-wife Suzy. Contact: SuzyBomp@AOL.com or write P.O.Box 7112, Burbank, CA 91510.

MARS BONFIRE
FORMER RESIDENCE
6383 Yucca
Hollywood

(Do Not Disturb Occupants)
In 1968, songwriter Mars Bonfire was living at this then (!) sleazy apartment. He had just moved to L.A. from Toronto with John Kay's band Sparrow, which broke up. Kay asked him to write a song for his new band, Steppenwolf, and being doubly inspired by a motorcycle poster at a head shop on Hollywood Blvd. and his recent acquisition of an old Ford Falcon, Bonfire penned "Born To Be Wild," which became one of Steppenwolf's signature songs (and prominently featured in the film *Easy Rider*). The song is also significant for containing the first musical application of the term "heavy metal," i.e. the "heavy metal thunder" roar of a motorcycle. Bonfire says he remembered the phrase from chemistry classes in school.

BONO'S RESTAURANT
1700 Indian Road
Palm Springs

Opened in 1985, this restaurant took root firmly in this glamorous desert town and Sonny Bono, the transplanted rock star

turned restaurateur, ultimately parlayed that popularity into the city's mayorship. During the early 1980s a previous Bono's enjoyed quite a bit of publicity, but less popularity, in West Hollywood. It was the subject of a flurry of pro and con letters in the Los Angeles Times regarding its northern Italian fare (Cher wrote in the restaurant's defense). Restaurants have always figured in Sonny's career. Twenty years earlier he was summarily ejected from a popular record industry hangout, an event that spurred a hit song (See MARTONI'S). Sonny Bono died in a skiing accident in 1998.

BRAVE NEW WORLD
(former location)
1644 Cherokee
Hollywood

Love, formerly The Grass Roots, established itself at this club, when it was located at 7307 Melrose, current home of The Groundlings Theater. After Love signed to Elektra in early 1966, the club moved to this location. Its large stage area afforded Frank Zappa's Mothers (the name was later lengthened to Mothers Of Invention by the record company) the opportunity to engage in 'theatrics' heretofore impossible. Zappa's Freak Out map called Brave New World "a very IN sort of late-teen spot."

BROTHER RECORDS

(former location)
1454 5th Street
Santa Monica

The Beach Boys formed their own record label, Brother Records, in 1967 but didn't open an office until 1973. The label made several recordings but issued only two albums: The Beach Boys *Smiley Smile* and the self-titled debut of the South African group Flame. The Brother Records logo, though, remained affixed to all Beach Boys records until 1980.

ROY BROWN GRAVE

Eternal Valley Memorial Park
Newhall

If Roy Brown had written only "Good Rockin' Tonight" it would be enough to label him great, but he also had a singing style that made him an early progenitor of rock and roll. Born in New Orleans in 1920, he sang in gospel groups as a youngster and honed a shouting and crying style that set the blues world on its ear in 1947 when he wrote and recorded "Good Rockin' Tonight." That hit, and the many that followed, propelled Brown to rhythm and blues stardom, allowing him to headline concerts around the country and tour lavishly with a fleet of Cadillacs. But then in the mid-fifties, rock and roll, the music he helped sire, pushed him out of the picture. (As did age—younger cats, most notably Jackie Wilson, copied his style and succeeded with it.) Brown lived in L.A. for nearly thirty years. In the late 1970s, he started working again in the U.S. and Europe, but just as he seemed on the brink of stardom he died suddenly of a heart attack near his San Fernando Valley home on May 21, 1981. At least he lived long enough to know there was a new generation of fans who loved him.

SOLOMON BURKE'S CHURCH

(former location)
46th & Compton
Los Angeles

In 1987 and 1988, Bishop Solomon Burke—known to the secular world as the popularizer of "Just Out Of Reach," "Down in the Valley," "Cry To Me," "If You Need Me," and "Everybody Needs Somebody to Love" (the latter three covered by The Rolling Stones)—held forth from this church. (One of the raucous services was videotaped for broadcast, but never aired, by TV producer Ken Erlich.)

BURNETTE BROTHERS GRAVES
Forest Lawn Cemetery
Glendale

John and Dorsey Burnette were hard-living brothers from Tennessee who set out to make it in the music business and succeeded. They vied for boxing careers in their hometown of Memphis in the early 1950s, and in 1954 both worked at Crown Electric Company (Elvis Presley also worked here at the time). But primarily the Burnette brothers were musicians. In 1955 they formed a band with fellow Crown employee Paul Burlison. That band, The Rock and Roll Trio, won first place on "Ted Mack's Amateur Hour" and was signed to Coral Records. Their records, now considered rockabilly classics (especially "Tear It Up"), flopped upon release despite the band's appearance in the film *Rock, Rock, Rock* (1956). In 1957, the battling

Burnettes—they were feisty fellows—moved to L.A., where they met Ricky Nelson. Nelson recorded their songs "Believe What You Say" and "Waitin' In School" and they entered a rock and roll circle that included Nelson, Gene Vincent and Eddie Cochran. In 1960 Dorsey had two hit records on his own, "(There Was a) Tall Oak Tree" and "Hey Little One" (later a hit for his chum Glen Campbell), and the next year Johnny followed with even bigger hits, "Dreamin'" and "You're Sixteen"

(covered in 1974 by Ringo Starr). Johnny drowned in a boating accident in 1974. Dorsey became successful in country music during the seventies, but died of a heart attack in 1979. (Johnny's son Rocky had his own hit, "Tired of Toein' the Line," in 1980. Dorsey's son Billy, after recording a couple of albums in the early 1980s, joined Fleetwood Mac in 1988.)

CANTER'S
419 N. Fairfax
Los Angeles

To look at it, you wouldn't think that this is the place Frank Zappa declared "The Top Freako Watering Hole and Social HQ." In the heart of "Kosher Canyon," Canter's has long served as a meeting place for rockers. On weekends, its two a.m. rush (when the nightclubs close) is truly prodigious. Canter's was a freak sanctuary during the tempestuous mid-1960s due to its evenhanded treatment of long-haired and short-haired customers. In 1966, when "sidewalk-clearing" was high on the LAPD's agenda, curfew and loitering arrests were frequently made here. During the early 1960s Phil Spector frequently occupied a booth here with Lenny Bruce. Today, Canter's continues to feed the local music community, drawing performers as diverse as U2 and Neil Diamond and the connecting Kibbitz Room hosts local bands (Jakob Dylan's Wallflowers "interned" here) and features a booth dedicated to longtime L.A. music scene figure Chuck E. Weiss.

CAPITOL RECORDS

1750 N. Vine
Hollywood

The "stack of records" building opened in 1955, thirteen years after the label's founding. It has been home to many hits. Just look at the lobby—the walls are festooned with gold records by The Beatles, Frank Sinatra, Glen Campbell, Helen Reddy, The Band, The Kingston Trio, Peggy Lee, Steve Miller, Pink Floyd, Les Paul and Mary Ford, Nat King Cole, Bob Seger, Duran Duran, The Beach Boys, Dean Martin and many others. Its still-operational recording studios reverberate with the history of music that has rocked the world. Today Capitol continues as a player in the tempest-tossed record business, making it easily the longest running Hollywood record company (more than 55 years). The light atop the Capitol Tower "needle" blinks H-O-L-L-Y-W-O-O-D in Morse Code. In December, the pole is draped with lights making an illuminated Christmas tree.

CARPENTERS APARTMENTS

We've Only Just Begun –
8345 5th St., Downey
Close To You–
8356 5th St., Downey

When Karen and Richard Carpenter hit it big in the seventies, they invested in the old neighborhood, building these across-the-street from each other apartments buildings and naming them after their two biggest hits. The song-naming penchant continues: Richard houses a collection of vintage cars in a building named "Yesterday Once More" in Downey. (Downey is a suburb ten miles south of downtown L.A. that has produced famous musicians over three decades. In the sixties The Chantay's did "Pipeline" on the now-defunct Downey label; the Carpenters emerged in the seventies; The Blasters broke through from Downey in the eighties and Downey is just a stone's throw (well, if Hercules threw it) from Hawthorne, where The Beach Boys grew up—See WENZEL'S.)

THE CASTLE
(former location)
4320 Cedarhurst Circle
Los Feliz

In 1966, Arthur Lee and his band Love lived in this rambling manse which was not the location of the first album's "rock" photos. (That stone formation, in a well-hidden Laurel Canyon location, has been demolished.) The song, "The Castle," appears on Love's *Da Capo* album, and a fanatical Love appreciation magazine, *The Castle*, is published in England.

CAT & FIDDLE
6530 Sunset Blvd.
Hollywood

British musician Kim Gardner (Creation, Byrds, Ashton, Gardner & Dyke) owns this British bistro in the heart of Hollywood with his wife Paula. It is not just a pub with dart boards and pints—though it is that—but a respected restaurant with English & American fare, on a large outdoor patio. Many British musicians (Gardner's old bandmate Ron Wood, for one) and sports figures make this a home away from home when they visit L.A. There is no set live-music policy though Jazz on Sundays and open-mike Mondays seem in place, but it is always interesting—for example, in mid-1997 Carlos Guitarlos debuted the Top Jimmyless Rhythm Pigs here.

CATHAY DE GRANDE
(former location)
Selma & Argyle
Hollywood

The Cathay de Grande was a Chinese restaurant turned punk nightclub that reigned during that music's heyday in the late seventies and early eighties. Blues (Roy Brown, Memphis Slim), punk (Black Flag), roots (The Blasters, Rose Maddox), and pop (The Go-Go's, The Knack) bands played in its dangerously crowded basement until the club closed in 1985. (It reopened briefly as the All

American Tavern later that year.) The Van Halen song "Top Jimmy" was written about the club's blues-belting mainstay, who, with his band the Rhythm Pigs, held sway here on Monday nights. (Top Jimmy got his name by working at Top Taco, across from A&M Records.) The Cathay's sign can be seen in the film *Eating Raoul* when Paul Bland is riding atop a truck at night.

THE CATHOUSE
(former location)
836 North Highland
Hollywood

This club, described by founder Riki Rachtman as "a rock and roll haven for decadents," was a slice of heavy metal heaven. Hard rockers in leather with big hair used to come here to meet girls in various states of dress and undress. This Tuesdays-only club operated for about four years and closed in the early 1990s.

THE CAVERN CLUB
(former location)
alley behind 6419 Hollywood Blvd.
Hollywood

The swinging "mod" scene burst forth anew in 1985 at this colorful but short-lived club. It started here in the old KFWB radio building as a sixties club called Rave-Up that was run by "King of Clubs" Larry Lazar. When Bomp Records maven Greg Shaw took over from Lazar shortly after its inception (Lazar moved on to other projects) he renamed it The Cavern, and installed deejay Audrey Moorehead (who later co-hosted the "It's Happening" TV show with Domenic Priore). The apparition of sixties-clad-and-coiffed teenagers dancing anew to "beat" records caught the fancy of the media and The Cavern was covered by People, Time, "Entertainment Tonight," and other news outlets. The Cavern closed after less than a year.

THE CENTRAL
(former location)
8852 Sunset Blvd.
West Hollywood

From 1969 to 1981 it was Filthy McNasty's nightclub (the old Filthy McNasty's awning can be seen in the upper-left corner of The Sweet's 1975 *Desolation Boulevard* album cover—See FM STATION). Prior to that it was The Melody Room. For many years The Central was a dependable work-horse bar for bands on the way up, and also a well-known jam club—Eric Burdon and John Belushi used to sit in, and many big stars did guest stints. Chuck E. Weiss and the Goddam Liars held forth every Monday to packed houses for more than six years, drawing a diverse swatch of show business revelers and savvy civilians. The Central was made up to be the London Fog for the Oliver Stone Doors movie, but this was not the location of that club—it was up the street, west of the Whisky (See BETWEEN CLARK AND HILLDALE). In 1993, actor Johnny Depp opened The Viper Room in this space (See THE VIPER ROOM).

CENTURY CITY
Santa Monica Blvd.
Avenue of the Stars
Los Angeles

Tom Petty sang "Don't Wanna Live In Century City" as a protest against the coldness of this Brasilia-like city, built on the former back lot of the 20th Century-Fox film studios (hence "Century" City, see?). This slab of pseudo-Manhattan is known for its tall buildings full of lawyers—perhaps that's why Petty thought it lacked warmth. (Petty's song was reportedly inspired by a visit with his idol, ex-Byrd Roger McGuinn, who once lived here.)

CHADNEY'S RESTAURANT
3000 W. Olive
Burbank

Not rock-historical on its own (its adjacency to NBC-TV doesn't concern us, this is a music book), it has been a regular gig site for two prominent LA session men, Earl Palmer and Emil Richards, who have performed here weekly for much of the 1980s and 1990s. Palmer is a jazz-based drummer whose rhythms have powered countless hit rock & roll records, starting in 1949 in his native New Orleans with Fats Domino's "The Fat Man." He played on most New Orleans hits of the early and mid 1950s, including virtually all by Fats, Little Richard, and Professor Longhair. In 1957 he moved to Los Angeles and became (permanently it seems) one of our town's most important percussionists, playing on records ranging from "La Bamba" and "You've Lost That Lovin' Feelin'" to 'class' acts like Sinatra and Diana Ross. Percussionist Emil Richards played on countless records in the 1960s and was an original member of Phil Spector's "Recking Crew."

RAY CHARLES' OFFICE (RPM PRODUCTIONS)
2107 W. Washington Blvd.
Los Angeles

Ray Charles runs his businesses from this office building, which also contains recording studios where he has made records since 1963. He has not done much outside production lately, but during the 1960s Charles recorded artists like Louis Jordan and Billy Preston here for his Tangerine label. Stevie Wonder, Glen Campbell, and Quincy Jones have recorded with Ray as well. (Don't show up here. Send a tape.)

CHATEAU MARMONT
8221 Sunset Blvd.
West Hollywood

A manor in the old-style manner, this space has long been a beacon to movie stars and also to rockers: Bob Dylan, Iggy Pop, Mick Jagger, Gram Parsons, Ringo Starr, and the Jefferson Airplane have been tenants. Barry Mann & Cynthia Weill wrote "You've Lost That Lovin' Feelin'" in the Chateau, and first played it for Phil Spector over a Chateau phone. Jim Morrison took his friend Danny Sugerman here to see drug-wracked Tim Hardin. (Later, when Morrison lived here, he hurt his back trying to swing from the roof into his window hanging onto a drain pipe.) John Lennon and Yoko Ono sometimes stayed in the nearby bungalows, Led Zeppelin rented them for orgies and, of course, in 1982 John Belushi died in one. In 1990, actor Bud Cort, a former tenant, co-directed a documentary film about the Chateau for German television. The rooms are old-worldly, and the lobby is too—the Chateau is the height of good taste and discretion.

"CHERISH" BIRTHPLACE
721 N. Alfred
West Hollywood

Association founding member Terry Kirkman was living in this apartment in 1965 when he had a decision to make: whether to watch the 11:00 news or write a song. He opted for the latter, and in a half hour composed "Cherish," ("The word had interested me for a long, long time," said Kirkman) which became the band's biggest record. (Two Association recordings rank in the 50 most-played songs of all time: "Cherish," and the Addrisi bothers' composition "Never My Love.")

CINNAMON CINDER
(former location)
11345 Ventura Blvd.
Studio City

This big teenage night club of the sixties was run by enterprising radio personality Bob Eubanks, who rose to TV fame as the host of "The Newlywed Game." In 1964 Eubanks presented The Beatles at the Hollywood Bowl, and it was here that The Beatles held their press conference before the show. Three Dog Night singer Danny Hutton remembers, as a teenager, being personally ejected by Eubanks when he was hanging around without the price of admission. The house band, The Pastel Six, scored a national hit with "Cinnamon Cinder," written for them (the

club predates the song) by Russ Regan (See WENZEL'S). There was also a Cinnamon Cinder in Long Beach. The site next became the Magic Mushroom (Firesign Theater did some memorable KPPC broadcasts from here); then the Point After sports bar; and then a country-music club called V.I.S. (purportedly Very Important Shitkicker), run by Dick Clark.

CIRO'S
(former location)
8433 Sunset Blvd.
West Hollywood

Now a legend in its own right as The Comedy Store, this building originally held Ciro's, a high-life club for the rich and famous from 1939 to its closing in 1957. In the early 1960s it reopened as the Crazy Horse, a twist club, featuring Donnie Brooks ("Mission Bell") as the house band. Next it reopened as Ciro's, and featured hot new acts like Sonny and Cher (part of their 1967 movie *Good Times* was shot here), The Lovin' Spoonful, and The Byrds (their first album's back cover shows them onstage here with Bob Dylan). By 1966 the name had changed to It's Boss, and the club held sway over teenyboppers with a regular menu of hot acts: Love, Tom Jones, Dino, Desi and Billy—and a fifteen-year-old age minimum(!) After the Sunset Strip fracas in late 1966, It's Boss reopened on February 22, 1967, with more mature music—Marvin Gaye was the first headliner, followed by Brook Benton, and The Fifth Dimension. It rode out the sixties with a variety of acts, including that of the temporary home of the psychedelic club Kaleidoscope (See AQUARIUS). From 1970 to 1976 Art Laboe ran his Oldies But Goodies club—the first of its kind in America (See ORIGINAL SOUND RECORDS)—here, and then the club was taken over by Sammy (later Mitzi) Shore's Comedy Store.

CLUB 88
(former location)
11784 Pico Blvd.
West Los Angeles

This was the west side equivalent of Hollywood's Cathay de Grande in the 1980s, the former strip-show house showcased rising bands, including The Go-Go's, The Bangles, The Blasters, and X. (Much of the X footage in Penelope Spheeris's punk documentary *The Decline of Western Civilization* was shot here.)

CLUB LINGERIE

6507 Sunset Blvd.
Hollywood

As Club Lingerie it has hosted The Plasmatics, The Replacements, Joe Turner, The Cramps, Sleepy La Beef, Foster and Lloyd—a diverse bag. During the seventies this was Souled Out, a soul nightclub. Many performers hung out here, including Tina Turner, Etta James, Kris Kristofferson, Bloodstone and Stevie Wonder (Motown had its office right across the street). During the 1960s it was The Red Velvet. Though The Kinks, Sonny and Cher, and The Turtles appeared here, The Red Velvet generally drew an older rock crowd for bands like The Righteous Brothers, The Bobby Fuller Four, and The Knickerbockers (the house band, whose "Lies" hit number twenty on the Billboard charts in 1966). As a result, it was summarily dismissed on Zappa's "freak" map as "HQ for the plastic & pompadour set." (Perhaps prophetically as a new "pompadour set" emerged in the 1980s at the club's "Rockabilly Wednesdays.") Going still further back, Eddie Cochran played here in 1959. And record producer Kim Fowley remembers coming to the KRLA Teen Night Club here in 1960 and seeing Eugene Church, Bobby Day and John and Judy (a brother-sister act from which John Maus and Scott Engel of The Walker Brothers emerged).

EDDIE COCHRAN GRAVE

Forest Lawn Cemetery
Cypress

Eddie Cochran's grave is little noted at the Cypress branch of the famed Forest Lawn cemetery chain, Karen Carpenter's nearby crypt well overshadows it. The beautiful relief-engraved headstone lies flat and attracts little attention—quite a contrast to what Cochran album annotator Lenny Kaye called "his mad dash through life." As a teenager in Bell Gardens, a factory city in south L.A., Eddie was constantly writing and singing. Like Buddy Holly, his earliest effort was in a country duo, with Hank Cochran (no relation). He recorded for small labels and appeared at record hops and school assemblies with deejay Art Laboe. Liberty Records in Hollywood signed Eddie in 1956, and a string of hits followed, including "Summertime Blues," "C'mon Everybody," and "Something Else." He also appeared in two seminal rock movies, *Untamed Youth* and *The Girl Can't Help It* (to which he was added at the last minute after the film company's negotiations with Elvis Presley fell through). Cochran led a rocker's lifestyle. He rode a motorcycle, and hung with Gene Vincent, Buddy Holly, Ricky Nelson, and Johnny and Dorsey Burnette (See GENE VINCENT, RICKY NELSON, BURNETTE BROTHERS).

His popularity in England was enormous—he was one of the few American rockers to tour there. On his U.K. tour in the spring of 1960 he traveled town-to-town like a Caesar in a triumphant motorcade flanked by his girlfriend, Sharon Sheeley (See SHARON SHEELEY), and fellow rocker Gene Vincent. But that was his final tour. On April 17, 1960, he, Sheeley, and Vincent were heading to Heathrow airport for their return flight to America when their taxicab skidded on a rain-slick road and crashed, killing Cochran and seriously injuring Sheeley and Vincent. Cochran's memory is still cherished in England and France (many rockers there sport his likeness in tattoos). The English film Radio On (1979) features Sting as a gas station attendant who works near the crash site and dedicates his life to Cochran.

COCOANUT GROVE
Ambassador Hotel
3400 Wilshire Blvd.
Los Angeles

Look quick—this venerable old nightclub, and the hotel that surrounds it, is scheduled for demolition (though as of 1998 its fate is still far from settled). The wrecker's ball will end a story that started in 1921, when The Ambassador opened as one of the classiest hotels in the world. Along with the splendid hostelry came the Cocoanut Grove, whose tropical-palm motif set the stage for elegant movie star parties. Even when times changed, the Ambassador moved with them and remained a top-notch venue throughout the 1960s (though it's most remembered, alas, for the killing of Robert Kennedy here in 1968). The Cocoanut Grove changed too. For a while it was the Now Grove with Sammy Davis, Jr. and it booked rock acts as well. On April 16, 1967, The Kaleidoscope temporarily set up shop here, calling itself the Banana Grove and presenting a bill that consisted of The Grateful Dead, Jefferson Airplane, and Canned Heat. Rock acts continued to appear sporadically through the 1970s— Ike and Tina Turner, Etta James, Waylon Jennings, Bonnie Raitt, The Boomtown Rats—but ultimately it just didn't work, and the Cocoanut Grove became inactive in the 1980s. It continues to be used for movies and videos. The televised Roy Orbison tribute with Bruce Springsteen and Elvis Costello was done here on October 30, 1987. (The Lovin' Spoonful do a song, "Coconut Grove," on their Hums of the Lovin' Spoonful album, but it's about a place in Florida).

NAT KING COLE FORMER HOME
401 South Muirfield
Hollywood
(Do Not Disturb Occupants)

When Nat King Cole moved into this luxurious home in the elegant Hancock Park area of L.A. in 1947, the residents revolted against "coloreds" moving in. Daughter Natalie Cole says she can remember seeing the word "nigger" burnt

into their lawn. Cole weathered this storm by going door to door and introducing himself to his neighbors. (It is said that a neighbor told him he was wary of "undesirables," and Cole said, "If I see any, I'll call you.") He died here in 1965. It is no longer the Cole family residence.

COLORADO BLVD.
Pasadena

Somewhat known for a flower-oriented parade each January 1st, its main significance to rock fans is as the drag-strip for "The Little Old Lady From Pasadena." This desolate west end of the boulevard would have been good for drag-racing. Not so good for racing, just a mile east, is Old Town, the "bohemian" district where you can enjoy mall chain stores in an outdoor setting. "LOL" lyricist Roger Christian (he also wrote lyrics for "Dead Man's Curve," "Drag City," "Little Deuce Coupe," "Don't Worry Baby" and others) was a popular KRLA deejay in the 1960s, who palled with Brian Wilson, Jan & Dean, and record producer Gary Usher. Christian died July 11, 1991.

CONTINENTAL HYATT HOUSE
(now Hyatt on Sunset)
8401 Sunset Blvd.
Hollywood

Unofficially dubbed "The Riot House," this place was THE rock and roll hotel in the 1970s:

 • Led Zeppelin rented as many as six floors here for their carryings on. Their partying set a standard that has never been equaled, with orgies, motorcycles in the halls, and stories yet untold.

 • Lemmy Kilminster, of Hawkwind, wrote "Motorhead" here.

 • The Rolling Stones movie *Cocksucker Blues* shows Keith Richards and Bobby Keyes throwing a television out of a window of this hotel.

 • Jim Morrison lived here until he was evicted by management for hanging out a window by his fingertips, dangling over the pavement (See CHATEAU MARMONT).

The 1970s management apparently courted the rock crowd. Legend has it that there was a full-sized photo of a long-haired musician behind the counter with the following written on it: "Treat This Man With Respect—He May Have Just Sold A Million Records." The place quieted down in the 1980s, but still gets its share of musicians: Little Richard, for one, lived here through much of the 1990s.

SAM COOKE DEATH SITE

Webb (née Polaris) Motel
9137 Figueroa
Los Angeles

Sam Cooke had everything—the voice, talent and looks that made him the hero of record buyers of all colors—so his death here in 1964 in an extramarital tryst was an especially heartbreaking fall from grace. America had lost a hero in a most unsavory way. Cooke was an angel-voiced gospel singer with the Chicago-based Soul Stirrers (a group that also spawned soul singer Lou Rawls) when he branched out into the secular world with "You Send Me" in 1957. That song rocketed to number one and for the next seven years he was never off the charts. Cooke's many big hits included "Cupid," "Chain Gang," "Twisting the Night Away," and the stirring civil rights-inspired ballad "A Change Is Gonna Come" that was released after his death. He was on top of the world on December 11, 1964, when he visited Martoni's Restaurant in Hollywood (See MARTONI'S), picked up Elisa Boyer, a twenty-two year old model, and took her back to his motel. He undressed and expected her to do the same, but she ran out into the street with his clothes. Cooke, nearly naked, ran to the manager's office and thinking Boyer was in there, pounded on the door and then broke in. The manger, taking him for a robber, shot him dead. He is buried in the Forest Lawn cemetery in Glendale.

THE COUNTRY CLUB

18415 Sherman Way
Canoga Park

Chuck Landis, whose Largo strip-show club was transformed into The Roxy, opened this enormous venue in 1974. The Country Club's fortunes rose and fell. For a while it was exclusively a country music venue—hence the name. Merle Haggard was the first act to play it and then it veered to rock. Promoter Jim Rissmiller leased it in 1978 and presented many rock shows, including The Boomtown Rats and Thin Lizzy. Under new management in the eighties it presented rock acts like Poison, Warrant, Michael Schenker, Mötley Crüe, REO Speedwagon, and U2. Today the site functions regularly as a rock club, but is inhibited, as The Starwood was (See STARWOOD), by neighbors' objections. Prince performed here in 1988 at a private party after the MTV Awards. Mick Jagger's 1988 video with Jeff Beck, "Throwaway," was shot here.

THE CRAMPS
FORMER RESIDENCE
1206 1/2 Edgemont
Hollywood
(Do Not Disturb Occupants)

Lux Interior and Poison Ivy, founders of The Cramps, lived in the right upstairs apartment here for most of the 1980s. The back cover of the single "Can Your Pussy Do the Dog" was shot in the living room. The band—which included drummer Nick Knox for more than ten years—moved to L.A. from New York around 1980. Their impassioned renderings of rockabilly and "trash" songs spawned the field of "psychobilly," which they reluctantly lead. The Cramps are seldom seen in public around L.A. and their zealously guarded privacy has had some extreme effects. Overeager fans have followed them and even sifted through their garbage. In 1987, a rumor that Lux was dead spanned the globe before being officially denied in Patrick Goldstein's column in the L.A. Times. The Cramps' worldwide following is ferocious—Cramps tattoos are common in France and England—but their American record output has been relatively sparse (3 U.S. albums between 1982 and 1997), unless you count the more than fifty Cramps bootleg albums that are out. The Cramps may be living in the L.A. area still, but no one knows—not even their record label.

DARBY CRASH DEATH SITE
137 N. Fuller
Hollywood
(Do Not Disturb Occupants)

Darby Crash (born Jan Paul Beahm) was the lead singer of L.A.'s most formidable punk band, The Germs, from 1977 until the group's disbanding in 1979. Onstage he displayed an animalistic rage, snarling bleak and hostile lyrics at breakneck speed, often covering himself in peanut butter or broken glass. But his pain apparently ran too deep to vent fully and on Sunday morning, December 7, 1980, he and his girlfriend Casey wrote suicide notes and took overdoses of heroin in a guest house behind her mother's house here. Casey survived, Darby didn't. (It is thought that Darby, who "fixed" the shots, deliberately underdosed Casey.) Darby's death was deeply felt in the Los Angeles punk community, but was overshadowed in the outside world by John Lennon's death the next day. Darby is buried at Holy Cross Cemetery, 5835 Slauson, in Culver City.

PEE WEE CRAYTON GRAVE
Inglewood Park Cemetery
720 East Florence
Inglewood

An influential blues guitarist and singer who moved to L.A. in 1935 (he was born December 18, 1914 in Liberty Hill, Texas), Connie Curtis "Pee Wee" Crayton was directly influenced by his

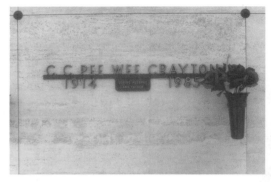

friend and teacher T-Bone Walker. He became a fixture on the burgeoning Central Avenue jazz scene in the forties, playing frequently at Johnny Otis's Barrelhouse. He also did session guitar work for Ivory Joe Hunter and other blues singers. Crayton recorded several blues hits in the late 1940s, including "Blues After Hours" and "Texas Hop," and toured the country with his own band. But his fortunes, like those of most musicians from that era, fell during the early fifties (despite Crayton's historical distinction as the first guitarist to use a Stratocaster, a new guitar prototype lent to him in 1954 by inventor Leo Fender) and he eased out of the music business temporarily, moving with his wife Esther and their daughter Peaches to Detroit in 1956, and then to Des Moines, Iowa, before resettling in L.A. in 1960. For much of the sixties Pee Wee made his living driving a truck, playing music only as a sideline. But at that decade's end he enjoyed renewed popularity through new recording contracts and an appearance on the Johnny Otis *Live at Monterey* album (1970). Through the seventies and early eighties Crayton played in L.A. and around the world, both as a soloist and as a guitarist for bluesmen like Roy Brown and Big Joe Turner. When Pee Wee died unexpectedly on June 25, 1985, he was a happy man, surrounded by a loving family and having lived long enough to see his music career blossom once again.

CROSBY, STILLS & NASH
ALBUM COVER SITE
(former location)
North of 809 Palm
West Hollywood

Photographer Henry Diltz posed David Crosby, Stephen Stills, and Graham Nash on the porch of a ramshackle dwelling on this lot in 1969 for their eponymous album, and when he saw the photos was pleased with the results—till someone pointed out they were

posed as Nash, Stills and Crosby. A week later they trekked back for a re-shoot and found the place demolished, so the wrong-order picture was used. (The fourth figure on the back cover, stripped in as an afterthought, was drummer Dallas Taylor, for whom Crosby, Stills Nash and Young did two 1990 benefit performances to aid him after an illness.) This site has long been a fenced-in parking lot.

DAIRY QUEEN

(former location)
Moorpark & Bakman
North Hollywood

Rock-documentary maker Malcom Leo (*The Beach Boys: An American Band* and *This Is Elvis*) worked here while attending North Hollywood High School. His classmates Dick & Don Addrisi came in one day in June, 1959 to celebrate the release of their first Del-Fi record, "Cherrystone," which made the na-tional charts. The Addrisi Brothers made their biggest impact as songwriters, penning "Never My Love" for the Association (the most-played song in the history of BMI). North Hollywood High, Leo tells us, hosts a huge reunion each year with entertainment by another of the school's famous musical alumni, the Mel-tones.

SAMMY DAVIS JR.'S FORMER RESIDENCE

8841 Evanview
West Hollywood
(Do Not Disturb Occupants)
This is the house in which The Band recorded their second al-bum *The Band* in 1969. That album was lavishly examined on an edition of the BBC-TV "Classic Albums" series.

DEAD MAN'S CURVE #1

Sunset, west from Groverton, across from Drake Stadium

This should be a bet-settler. Ev-eryone in L.A. seems to have his or her own idea of where the curve described in the 1964 Jan and Dean song "Dead Man's Curve" is located, but no one knows better than the song's co-writers, Dean Torrence, Roger Christian and Jan Berry (fourth writer Brian Wilson wasn't queried) who all agree that this is the spot. In January of 1961, comedian Mel Blanc suffered a near-fatal car crash here, which spurred the city to regrade the curve—so in fact, Dead Man's Curve doesn't really exist anymore. (Incidentally, the fatal Ernie Kovacs car crash in 1962 occurred on a straight stretch of Santa Monica Blvd. southwest of the Beverly Hills Hotel.)

DEAD MAN'S CURVE #2

Sunset, just west of Whittier
Beverly Hills

Jan Berry of Jan and Dean suffered a near-fatal car crash near here in 1966. Driving his new Corvette Stingray, Berry was nearly killed in a collision with a garbage truck. Jan and Dean, the California surf-singing duo, had enjoyed a long string of hits including "Drag City," "Sidewalk Surfin'," and "The Little Old Lady (From Pasadena)." Jan's accident was bitter irony—in Jan and Dean's 1964 hit "Dead Man's Curve" the song's hero crashes his Stingray on a curve and dies. Jan didn't die, but Jan and Dean's career was put on a long hold while he struggled to recover from head injuries. They returned to the stage in the 1970s, first surfacing at Jim Pewter and Bill Liebowitz's 1973 Surf Revival show at the Hollywood Palladium, and continue to perform together today.

You still could call this the real Dead Man's Curve. The song's lyrics describe a westbound race down Sunset, starting at Vine and crossing La Brea, Crescent Heights and Doheny—all the way to the unspecified curve. A look at the map shows that after Doheny the road takes gentle curves through Beverly Hills, then suddenly slams right at a wall just past Whittier. One wonders how racers could pass that obstacle and the series of s-curves that follow it (the ones between Charing Cross and Carolwood were also rebanked, leading to speculation that they, too, were "the" Dead Man's Curve), just to finish the race at the severe, but not demonstrably worse turn, at Groverton. Who knows? Dead Man's Curves have been spotted around L.A. more often that the monster has in Loch Ness. If you've been calling some curve near your house Dead Man's Curve, keep at it—who's to say you're wrong?

DEL-FI RECORDS

(former location)
6277 Selma
Hollywood

When Ritchie Valens' "Donna" and "La Bamba" became hits of Del-Fi Records late in 1958, owner Bob Keene moved the label's headquarters to this office above the California Bank. (Keene's residence at 1823 Dillon, where "Donna" was recorded, has been razed.) The location was fortunate: the bank had an unused basement vault which they allowed Keene to use for an echo chamber. In this office, Bobby Fuller recorded "I Fought the Law" for Keene's Mustang label early in 1966. Several years later, when the office was converted to Mystic Sound, these chambers were utilized to get just the right sound on Led Zeppelin's "Whole Lotta Love."

DELONGPRE PARK
Delongpre & Cherokee
Hollywood

One day in 1961, determined songwriter Jerry Fuller took a world atlas to this park and wrote a song he thought would be good for Sam Cooke. He walked over to Cooke's SAR Records office (See HOLLYWOOD PACIFIC BUILDING) and presented it to Cooke's representative Bumps Blackwell, who passed. Rick Nelson bassist Joe Osborne overheard Fuller's song in the hall, and asked if he could take it to Nelson. Fuller said sure, Nelson liked it, and the song, "Travelin' Man," went on to become Nelson's biggest-selling record.

DE NEVE PARK
Parkwood & Beverly Glen
Beverly Hills

During the early 1960s, Elvis Presley's football team used to battle Rick Nelson's football team on Sundays in this park. Both stars actually risked life and limb, slightly, in these hands-on games. (Johnny Rivers and Dean Torrence of Jan and Dean also sometimes played here on teams that challenged Elvis.) Unlike normal touch-football games, theirs were attended by a fleet of limos and a large crowd of spectators. Both sides had distinctions: Elvis' was manned by his cadre of Memphis buddies, and Rick's team contained several college and professional footballers. It was a symbolic Clash of the Titans and one in which Ricky had the edge. No scorecards were filled, nor records kept—but where are the home movies?

THE DERBY
Los Feliz & Hillhurst
Hollywood

Opened in 1993, the Derby was first famed for having the old Brown Derby restaurant's hat upon its roof, then prospered under a booking policy that encouraged happening local roots and jump-blues revivalist bands like Big Sandy, Royal Crown Revue, Big Bad Voodoo Daddy, Jimmy (Intveld) & The Gigolos, Russell Scott, and touring bands such as The Big 6 and The New Morty Show. The Derby was featured prominently in the movie *Swingers*.

DEVONSHIRE DOWNS
(former location)
Northridge

Now absorbed into Cal State Northridge grounds, this former horse track saw many rock shows during the sixties and seventies. Especially memorable was the two-day Newport '69 festival featuring The Animals, Jethro Tull, The Chambers Brothers and Jimi Hendrix. (Hendrix was plagued by equipment problems the first day, so to compensate his fans he played behind the other acts the second day.) The Country Fest '74 here featured Jerry Lee Lewis, Waylon Jennings and thirty other bands. Many new bands played here during the eighties, including Fear, Black Flag, Panther Burns, The Cramps and The Dickies.

DICK CLARK PRODUCTIONS
3003 Olive
Burbank
(No tours / No visitors)

"The world's oldest teenager" operates from this old house near NBC-TV. Clark started out as host of "American Bandstand" in 1957, and metamorphosed into a TV personality and mogul. Through the effort of Clark and people around him, rock and roll grew from the simple, honest, heartfelt music it once was to the big business it is today. Though "American Bandstand" is off the air, Clark's company still oversees music, movie and television enterprises from here.

DIMENSION RECORDS
(former location)
where Cole and Cahuenga split
south of Sunset
Hollywood

Dimension Records, which flourished briefly in the early 1960s with hits by Little Eva, Carole King, Big Dee Irwin and Tracy Dey was located upstairs here in the early 1960s. Reprise Records also maintained offices here around the same time.

DIONYSUS RECORDS
(former location)
433 E. Tujunga
Burbank

Founder Lee Joseph began Dionysus Records in this small house in Burbank in 1984. It continues to be one of the most successful "mom & pop" (Joseph runs it with his wife Aime) labels, and one of the most eclectic, releasing both new music (Big Sandy, Johnny Legend, Boss Martians) and reissues. In 1995 it moved to an actual office (!) in Burbank where, like Millie's restaurant (See MILLIE'S), you're likely to find musicians and journalists packing boxes and pushing brooms.

"DISGRACELAND"
(former location)
1553 Cassil
Hollywood
(Do Not Disturb Occupants)

In hippie days this would have been called a crash pad; in the eighties it was called Disgraceland. With one long-term resident, Pleasant Gehman of The Screamin' Sirens, this was a place for musicians to bop, flop and drop as they visited or partied through Hollywood. Residents included nearly all The

Go-Go's (when *Beauty and the Beat* hit number one, Belinda Carlisle was still living here.) Guests included Billy Idol, Lydia Lunch, Levi Dexter, members of Madness, Split Enz, Guns N' Roses, X, Fishbone, The Red Hot Chili Peppers, The Gun Club, The Specials, The Blasters and countless others. This apartment, owned by Jayne Mansfield's widower Mickey Hargitay, can be seen in the films *The Boost* and *The Running Kind*.

DOLPHIN'S OF HOLLYWOOD
(former location)
1065 East Vernon
Los Angeles

Starting in 1953, deejay Dick "Huggy Boy" Hugg began broadcasting a live rhythm and blues radio show from the window of a twenty-four hour record store (ingeniously named "Dolphin's of Hollywood" when it was culturally and geographically miles from there), bringing John Dolphin's record store and record company unparalleled exposure. The frantic bleating of Joe Houston's sax blaring "All Night Long" while Huggy Boy hollered, "Keep alive and listen in!"

was a Pied Piper's call for the restless teenagers of L.A., and soon the corner of Central and Vernon was the center of the emerging rock and roll culture. Dolphin's prevailed as one of the city's top record stores throughout the 1950s, and his record labels, Recorded In Hollywood (which wasn't), Cash, Money and Lucky, cut rhythm and blues sides by Houston, Pee Wee Crayton, Ernie Freeman and others. Dolphin also cut rock and roll with Bobby Day, Jesse Belvin and Eddie Cochran—right up until February 1, 1958, when songwriter Percy Ivy, unhappy at not receiving royalties on a song Dolphin had recorded, shot him dead in his office at 1248 South Berendo. (Future Beach Boy, Bruce Johnston, and future "Teen Beat" drummer Sandy Nelson were witnesses to the shooting. The teenagers were in Dolphin's office to play him their new demo.) Huggy Boy went on to become one of the city's best-loved and longest-enduring "oldies" deejays, and can still be heard on KRLA. Dolphin's continued operating for several years after its founder's death, but closed in the 1970s.

DOORS OFFICE
(former location)
8512 Santa Monica Blvd.
West Hollywood
The Doors' management conducted their business from this office near the corner of La Cienega in the late 1960s. The downstairs portion was the recording studio in which the band recorded the *L.A. Woman* album.

DOOTO MUSIC CENTER
(former location)
135th & Central
Los Angeles
This large hall owned by Dootsie Williams of DooTone Records has seen some great shows by Bobby Blue Bland, Little Milton and many other blues greats. The hall was torn down in 1997, following Williams death.

DOOTONE RECORDS
(former location)
9512 South Central
Los Angeles

Ex-bandleader, Dootsie Williams ran the DooTone label from this house starting in 1951. DooTone's first big hit, in February 1955 was "Earth Angel" by The Penguins (See EARTH ANGEL). DooTone followed up with lesser-selling but not less memorable hits by Don Julian and The Meadowlarks and Vernon Green and The Medallions. Williams switched to recording comedy in the 1960s, releasing a barrage of "party" albums by Redd Foxx.

DORE RECORDS
1608 Argyle
Hollywood

Once and still the home of Lew Bedell's eclectic and long-lived record label. Bedell, a New York tv show host in the early 1950s, moved to LA in 1955 to become partner with his cousin, Liberty Records co-founder Herb Newman, in the newly-formed Era Records, which scored early with two Gogi Grant hits, "Suddenly There's a Valley" and "The Wayward Wind" (written by Newman). When they severed their partnership in 1959, Bedell opened Dore Records in this office, on what was then "record row" on Argyle, and immediately hit gold with the Teddy Bears' "To Know Him Is To Love Him." He has continued issuing music ever since, as well as his own standup comedy tape, *Who The Hell Is Lew Bedell?*.

DRESDEN ROOM
1760 N. Vermont
Los Feliz

This place is testament to the fact that if you wait around long enough, the light of hipness will shine on you. The Dresden is a piano-bar adjoining a restaurant (whose main fare, go figure, is Italian food—Dresden is a town in Germany) whose mainstays Marty (bass/drums) & Elayne (piano/vocals) have apparently withstood all musical changes since 1959 with aplomb and pluck, singing smokey lounge tunes to an ever-shifting audience. In the late 1980s they were "discovered" by a new young, eager-for-change rock audience who constituted, then and now, a fan base that has kept the place packed every night. (Check out Marty and Elayne performing "Stayin' Alive" in the film *Swingers*.) The unanswerable question is: did Marty & Elayne anticipate the martini/lounge music movement or create it?

DUKE'S COFFEE SHOP
8909 Sunset Blvd.
Hollywood

Its t-shirts still say "Dukes at the Tropicana," harking back to its heyday adjoining the famed rock and roll hotel (See TROPICANA). During the sixties and seventies its adjacency to that hotel made Duke's a great place for musicians to meet and eat. Located next to The Whisky-A-Go-Go, it still draws a music-oriented clientele

(big crowds on weekends) with pretty much the same food and atmosphere—you still sit barracks-style with strangers, which often makes for new friendships.

DUNBAR HOTEL
4225 South Central
Los Angeles

During World War II, this was the northern border of a strip of black nightclubs that stretched to 48th Street and beyond. Every major figure in black culture visited or performed at any of a dozen highlife nightspots on Central, especially The Club Alabam, which adjoined the Dunbar. Paul Robeson, Joe Louis, W. E. B. DuBois, Louis Armstrong, Cab Calloway, Billie Holiday, Wynonie Harris, Duke Ellington, T-Bone Walker, Count Basie, Louie Jordan, Ella Fitzgerald, Lena Horne—everyone who was anyone visited Central Avenue and inevitably stayed or dined at the Dunbar. However, the end of the war pulled the plug on the glory that was Central. The Dunbar Hotel was built in 1928 as a hotel for black visitors—L.A. was a lot like Mississippi in those days—but fell into decay in the 1950s. Though the hotel was renovated in 1988 by owner Bernard Johnson with aims to make it a far-reaching black culture center (the building is already listed as a national monument), today it is called The Dunbar Apartments and houses senior citizens. A museum is being planned for the mezzanine.

"EARTH ANGEL" SITE
2190 W. 30th
Los Angeles
(Do Not Disturb Occupants)

During the early 1950s, mailman Ted Brinson, a former big-band bassist, had a small recording studio in this garage, in which DooTone Record president Dootsie Williams made demos. When Brinson told Williams his nephew had a singing group, The Penguins, Williams offered to produce their record here, and issue it on DooTone if it turned out well. The result was "Earth Angel." Williams took it to top deejay Huggy Boy, who played it on his radio show (See DOLPHIN'S OF HOLLYWOOD) and within weeks of its release in early 1955, it shot to the top of the charts. "Earth Angel" was a black breakthrough record. After it became a R&B hit, The Crew-Cuts, a white Canadian singing group, dutifully cut a cover version for the white market (as they had done with "Sh-Boom" by The Chords a year earlier). And although The Crew-Cuts' version made it all the way to number three, The Penguins' original sold nearly as well, getting up to number eight—a startling showing, and a sign that black artists could appeal to white buyers too. Besides standing as a musical national treasure, "Earth Angel" is a prime example of the overlooked field of West Coast doo-wop. Others bands recorded here too, including The Medallions, and Don Julian and The Meadowlarks. The garage is now used for storage.

ELECTRO-VOX RECORDING STUDIO
5546 Melrose
Hollywood

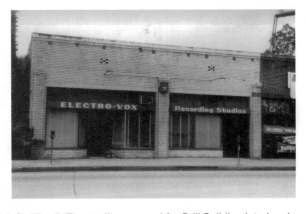

Opened in 1931 by Bert Gottschalk (son Alan still runs it), this place saw plenty of Hollywood movie activity, but our interest in it stems from two great rock records recorded here in the 1950s: "You Cheated" by The Shields (did you think that was an East Coast record?) and Sammy Masters' masterful rockabilly classic, "Pink Cadillac." (The studio was used for Brill Building interiors in the film *Grace Of My Heart*.) It is the only one-track mono-only studio still active in Hollywood.

ELEKTRA/ASYLUM RECORDS
(former location)
962 N. La Cienega
West Hollywood

Elektra Records was a folk-oriented New York label founded in the 1950s by Jac Holzman. In the mid-sixties they opened an L.A. office, and struck paydirt with The Doors. Asylum Records

was founded in 1970 by manager David Geffen, and it did well with Jackson Browne, Joni Mitchell, and Linda Ronstadt. When the labels merged in 1973 they forged a latter-day folk-rock axis that took hold of America. Then around 1979 the well went dry. Punk rock might have had some effect on tastes, or maybe people that age stopped buying records. In any case, the label folded its tent, left this exquisite building (you should see its central spiral staircase—with the skylight it looks like the stairway to heaven!), and relocated to an office building on Sunset.

EXODUS CLINIC
DANIEL FREEMAN HOSPITAL
4650 Lincoln
Marina Del Ray
Kurt Cobain walked away from the drug-rehab clinic here and flew to Seattle where he shot himself on April 6, 1994.

FARMER JOHN COMPANY
Soto & Vernon
Vernon

The Farmer John meat-packing plant is several blocks around, its walls and fences covered by barnyard murals. The cover of Dr. John's *Gumbo* album (1972) was shot in front of a portion of the mural that has remained unchanged to this day. "Farmer John" by The Premiers, an East L.A. band, was a hit in 1964, reaching number nineteen on the national charts. Los Lobos covered it in 1982 on an independently released single and Neil Young covered in on his 1990 *Ragged Glory* album.

FIVE-FOUR BALLROOM
54th & Broadway
Los Angeles

If these walls could talk... A hallowed location for R&B from the late 40s until the mid-1970s, this south-central L.A. landmark rivaled The Dunbar Hotel, in the glory of the performers who've graced its stage: Ray Charles, Bobby Bland, Wynonie Harris, Roy Milton, The Stax Revue. It was

L.A.'s answer to the Apollo. Hard times and shifting audience demographics conspired to close the place nearly 30 years ago, and a mid-1990s "re-birth" with old-time acts such as Clarence Frogman Henry and Charles Brown failed to rekindle its glory, despite the efforts of people including Percy Mayfield's widow Tina Mayfield and oldtime Fats Domino bandleader Billy Diamond.

FLASH CADILLAC FORMER RESIDENCE

616 S. Wilton
Los Angeles
(Do Not Disturb Occupants)

Was this the model for *Animal House* or is the similarity just coincidental? In 1973, high on their successful appearance as a high school band in *American Graffiti*, Colorado-based Flash Cadillac and the Continental Kids moved their fifties-style band to Los Angeles and set up in this old house just north of Wilshire. The living room was "animal chic." Beer cans were stacked in sculpture-like arrangements, and a photo of Annette Funicello dominated the mantle. There was a pool table in the dining room, and visitors in varying states of consciousness were strewn everywhere around the three-story, ten-room house. Flash and The Kids reigned supreme here for three years, entertaining visitors including Henry Winkler, Mike Love, Donny Most, Rob Reiner, Kim Fowley (who produced their music for *American Graffiti*), and Screamin' Lord Sutch. They got another movie role—two three-week trips to the Philippines resulted in a fraction-of-a-second appearance in *Apocalypse Now*—but when they got to feeling homesick (i.e., sick of their home), they moved back to Colorado. Now based in Colorado Springs, they still record and play, blazing a new career in the 1990s by performing with symphony orchestras around the country as well as club and convention dates.

FLIPPER'S ROLLER DISCO

(former location)
Santa Monica & La Cienega
West Hollywood

Formerly a bowling alley, this was a converted to a roller rink/disco by Shelter Records founder Denny Cordell in 1979, just at the end (thank goodness!) of the roller disco craze. Bands would play in the center "island" while skaters circled around them. Shades of The Buddy Holly

Story! The ill-fated facility hosted some mighty interesting acts, though. Who can forget Prince, wearing only a long coat and black jockstrap, with his band on a special stage at the north end of the rink? Let's not forget John Cougar's concert here in his semi-glitter period. And The Blasters were playing Flipper's one night in early 1980 when three members of Queen saw them and added them as the opener for the remaining dates of their West Coast tour. Flipper's petered out of existence by 1981. For a while there was talk of Motown erecting a building on this spot, but it never happened.

FM STATION
(former location)
Lankershim & Victory
North Hollywood
When club owner Filthy McNasty (this club's name is a reference to the owner's initials) uprooted the club that bore his name in Hollywood (See THE CENTRAL) in 1980, he fell back on this club, which he had run since 1974. It had other names before, including Hag's Place (as Merle Haggard's unsuccessful attempt to unseat The Palomino in the mid-1970s). FM Station was a popular showcase for local rock bands as well as national ones (The Band, Edgar Winter, Leon Russell, Nina Hagen). The club changed into a Mexican cantina in 1993.

FOLK MUSIC CENTER
220 Yale
Claremont

A music store snug on a tasteful street in a college town, the Folk Music Center's customers have included Jackson Browne, Taj Mahal, Leo Kottke, Ry Cooder, Joan Baez, and, going back, Jean Ritchie, Elizabeth Cotton and Mississippi John Hurt. From 1957 to 1959 the owners, the Chase family (psych-folkster Ben Harper is their grandson), also ran a folk club in Claremont called The Gold Ring, in which the Reverend Gary Davis, John Fahey, and a very young David Lindley played. (The Chases have recently revived The Gold Ring at Village Dance Arts on Harvard Place). The Folk Music Center is also a state-certified music museum with ancient and rare instruments displayed right alongside ones you can buy.

FOOTHILL CLUB
1922 Cherry Ave
Signal Hill

This Long Beach-surrounded town is famous for two things — an exceptionally enthusiastic police force and this club, operating continuously and owned by the Price family since the 1940s. The walls feature photos of Johnny Cash (autographed around 1960), Johnny Western, Billy Mize, Merle Haggard and The Collins Kids, making this one of LA's unheralded museums. In the olden days it was host to greats including Rose Maddox and Hank Williams. Today they book roots rockers such as Link Wray, Russell Scott, Big Sandy, and anything that fits. They are the holders of the oldest liquor license in L.A.

THE FORUM
Manchester Boulevard & Prairie Ave.
Inglewood

Started as a general purpose arena in the mid-1960s, it began hosting rock bands as soon as it became evident they could fill the place. The 17,000-seat venue has hosted The Rolling Stones, Bruce Springsteen, Led Zeppelin, Elvis Presley— you get the picture It is also the home of Lakers basketball, rodeos, moto-cross races, etc. (The name is now prefaced by the current advertisers name, The Great Western Forum; next year it could be the Coca-Cola Forum.)

FOSTER'S FREEZE
11969 Hawthorne
Hawthorne

Local legend has it that it was at this burger stand that young Brian Wilson saw a girl driving her daddy's T-Bird, which was subsequently taken from her, inspiring the song "Fun, Fun, Fun." Apocryphal? Perhaps, but it's certain that the adolescent Wilson boys spent plenty of time here, since it is just around the corner from their family home at 3701 W. 119th Street (which is torn down now).

FOX VENICE THEATER
(former location)
620 Lincoln Avenue
Venice

When this place was operating full-throttle in the mid-1970s, it was the cultural center for post-hippies. There were revival movies, surf movies, television festivals, Cajun documentaries narrated by Les Blank, love-ins, shove-ins—and music, including one "multi-media theatrical musical troupe" called the Mystic Knights of the Oingo Boingo. Their shows, here and at other like locations around L.A., were a dazzling hodgepodge of film clips, skits, money suits, magic, and music. During the latter days of the seventies (and of the theater) The Fox Venice ran excellent concerts, often in conjunction with McCabe's Guitar Shop (See McCABE'S), presenting Little Feat, Big Joe Turner, Bonnie Raitt, and John Lee Hooker (who recorded Live at the Fox Venice with Canned Heat). But still it fell victim to—what? Not progress; the area hasn't improved much. And you can't imagine there's ever been a lack of hippies in Venice. Maybe it was time for it to fold when cross-town enthusiasts—Venice's answer to Manhattan's "bridge and tunnel crowd"—got tired of driving there. The Mystic Knights of the Oingo Boingo, on the other hand, moved with the times, paring their name down to Oingo Boingo and catapulting to worldwide fame in the 1980s.

FRANKLIN CANYON
atop Coldwater Canyon

When you see The Rolling Stones' 1966 *Big Hits (High Tide and Green Grass)* album cover, it's natural to assume the foresty pictures were taken in England—but not so. Photographer Guy Webster dragged them up to Franklin Canyon, near his house, for the session. The back cover shows them in a ravine that is now paved over. The front cover has them posed at the edge of the same Franklin Reservoir that's there today. That album was, for a while, cloaked in controversy. Stone's manager Andrew Loog Oldham announced that its title would be "Could They Walk on Water?", but the title was changed at the last minute. This is how Oldham explains it in a "Factotainment" he wrote for his book entitled Making Pictures in Hollywood: "The pictures were great and plenty and one of Guy's shots against the water suggested to me the same image captured years later by Hal

Ashby with Peter Sellers at the end of *Being There*. I announced to the press that The Stones' next L.P. would be entitled "Could You Walk on the Water?" I felt that it may be deemed sacrilegious to take a position on this matter, but acceptable when put as a question. The group's then U.K. distributor, Decca, didn't agree, which was alright by me as I didn't have an album I could call Could You Walk on the Water? We got a lot of free press, and away with the title *Big Hits (High Tide and Green Grass)*, guess Everybody Must Get Stoned. Hooray for Hollywood, and dreams that come true." And did you assume Simon and Garfunkel's *Sounds of Silence* album cover was shot somewhere in upstate New York? Webster did that one here too, on Franklin Canyon Road, on a portion that is now paved.

FRED C. DOBBS COFFEE HOUSE
(former location)
8537 Sunset Blvd.
West Hollywood

Named after Humphrey Bogart's character in *The Treasure of Sierra Madre,* this was where the Sunset Strip people met in the mid-1960s (Phil Spector met Bob Dylan here, according to Billy James). Convenient to the Strip and Ben Frank's, the place served food and coffee and had a good jukebox. (Legend has Dylan hearing Ray Charles's "Let's Go Get Stoned" here and then writing "everybody must get stoned" in "Rainy Day Women #2 & #35." But you know how reliable legends are.) By 1966 a Frank Zappa pamphlet complained that "the Dobbs" had lost its cool because of outsiders crowding in. "The ruins are located at 8537 Sunset," it said.

FROLIC ROOM
6245 Hollywood Blvd.
Hollywood

Another struggling-musicians hangout in Hollywood, near Vine St. that's proved so popular it's spawned three nearby spin-offs. It was a convenient watering hole for acts playing at the Pantages down the street, or for the overflow from Raji's. An original Hirschfeld mural is mute testimony to the bar's heyday when this was the entertainment world's main intersection. Its facade is frequently shown in travelogues, commercials and record covers. The cover of the 1995 *Danny & Dusty* album (featuring members of Long Riders, Green & Red, Dream Syndicate) was shot here.

BOBBY FULLER DEATH SITE
1776 Sycamore
Hollywood

Twenty-four year old Bobby Fuller's body was found here on July 18, 1966, in front of the apartment he shared with his mother. Police ruled his death suicide "by inhalation of gasoline." Pretty funny conclusion? Pretty funny business, this death. Fuller had a top ten hit in 1965 with "I Fought the Law," a remake of an unknown post-Buddy Holly Crickets song, and was enjoying similar success with another Crickets cover, "Love's Made a Fool of You," when he died. He was born and reared in Texas, but had lived in L.A. for several years at the time of his death. Speculation ran riot at the time about what or whom Fuller had crossed to warrant being murdered—sorry, committing suicide—in this gruesome manner. But the matter remains unsolved (unless you accept the official explanation).

SLIM GAILLARD'S RECORD SHOP
(former location)
2122 W. Jefferson
Los Angeles

In the late 1940s, bop-talking, hitmaking ("Cement Mixer Putty Putty"), multi-instrumentalist Slim Gaillard had a record store at this location, which now houses a barber shop. Gaillard's ads swingingly described the store's location as "in the heart of Voutville."

GARDNER STREET SCHOOL
Hawthorn & Gardner Streets
Hollywood

Michael Jackson went to school here in the early 1970s. The school honored its most famous alumnus in October 1989, by naming its auditorium after him in a ceremony he attended.

GAS LITE CLUB
2030 Wilshire Blvd.
Santa Monica

Where did the original rockabilly guys go? One, Jackie Lee Waukeen Cochran, held forth here Friday and Saturday nights for more than ten years. Cochran's 50s recordings of "Mama Don't You Think I Know"/"Ruby Pearl" and "Buy A Car," brilliant, little-selling shots of red-hot rockabilly, are cherished today by fans throughout the world. His longevity at this club, which counts many college students as its base, proved that you don't have to be modern to be au courant. Cochran died suddenly March 15, 1998.

MARVIN GAYE DEATH SITE
2101 South Gramercy
Los Angeles
(Do Not Disturb Occupants)

When world-renowned soul singer/sex symbol Marvin Gaye got into an argument with his minister father, Marvin Gaye, Sr., at their plush home here on the night of April 1, 1984, the senior Gaye put an end to the fight with a bullet to his son's temple. The father was remanded to a mental institution, where he lived out his remaining years. Gaye was Motown's sex symbol from its beginning back in Detroit in the early sixties. He married label founder Berry Gordy's sister, but, embittered by their vicious divorce, moved to Belgium in the late 1970s. (He dedicated an album to his alimony payments called *Here, My Dear.*) Gaye returned to America in 1984, and was making a mighty comeback with the song "Sexual Healing" when he died.

GAZZARRI'S
(former location)
9039 Sunset Blvd.
West Hollywood

Owner Bill Gazzarri first opened his club at 319 N. La Cienega, presenting artists like The Standells, Jackie DeShannon and The McCoys (plus Johnny Rivers, whom he hired away from a club downtown, only to lose him to The Whisky). Moving up here in the mid-1960s, he snared The Doors, The

Byrds, Buffalo Springfield, and many other up-and-coming acts (including The Walker Brothers, who made their name here and then left for England, where they became huge stars). During the 1966 Sunset Strip "riots," Gazzarri led the fight against the city when it wanted to close all rock clubs. During the seventies this was the "other" rock club (though Van Halen played here a lot), somehow second to The Starwood and The Whisky. But during the eighties it came back into its own as one of the premiere hard rock showcases, the club marking the western end of a hard-rock strip that extends east to the Whisky. In 1996, the Gazzarri's building was gutted and re-opened as Billboard Live.

GEFFEN RECORDS
9130 Sunset Blvd.
Beverly Hills

This label was founded by David Geffen, who once co-managed (with Elliot Roberts) Joni Mitchell, Jackson Browne, Neil Young and Crosby, Stills and Nash from this very office. In 1970 he started the Asylum record label (The Eagles, Tom Waits, Joni Mitchell, Linda Ronstadt, Jackson Browne— See ELEKTRA/ASYLUM), and then in 1980 founded Geffen, which has proven successful with Guns N' Roses, Don Henley, Whitesnake, Aerosmith and others. Phil Spector Productions operated out of this building during the 1960s and 1970s. (Like all record companies, they don't want you showing up at the door. If you've got a song, send 'em a tape.)

THE GOLD CUP RESTAURANT
(former location)
Hollywood & Las Palmas
Hollywood

Once a beacon for teenage runaways, The Gold Cup attracted the worst elements of Hollywood Boulevard sleaze:

• Jackson Browne alludes to it in his song "On the Boulevard," referring to "The Golden Cup."

• Local band Black Randy and the Metro Squad recorded a song "Trouble at the Cup."

• In the late seventies there was a punk band called Arthur J and the Gold Cups, incorporating the names of two of the town's most unsavory restaurants. (Arthur J's, on Highland Ave., was torn down long ago.)

GOLD STAR RECORDING STUDIOS
(former location)
Santa Monica & Vine
Hollywood

Founded in 1950 by Dave Gold and Stan Ross (hence the name GOLD STAn R), who then added Stan's sound engineer cousin Larry Levine, Gold Star rose from a demo studio to possibly the most famous recording studio in the world. Phil Spector helped. In 1958, when Phil was a high-school kid coming in to record "To Know Him Is To Love Him" with The Teddy Bears, Gold Star had plenty of hits under its belt, but wasn't exactly famous. When Spector came back a few years later and created "Da Doo Ron Ron" and "And Then He Kissed Me" with The Crystals, "Be My Baby" with The Ronettes and "You've Lost That Lovin' Feelin'" with The Righteous Brothers, Gold Star went on the map all over the world. Spector shoved sometimes as many as twelve pianos into the small, apparently elastic-walled studio, and as many cellos—in addition, six bass players were not uncommon—to make a massive "wall of sound" that other producers flocked to Gold Star to get, but couldn't—the ambiance was Gold Star's, but it was Spector's genius that made the sound. Still, a lot of other hits were made here: "The In Crowd" by Dobie Grey, "Good Vibrations" by The Beach Boys, "The Lonely Bull" by Herb Alpert and The Tijuana Brass, "Summertime Blues" by Eddie Cochran, "La Bamba" by Ritchie Valens, "I Got You Babe" by Sonny and Cher, and many, many more. Gold Star was sold in 1983 when a shopping mall urgently needed to be born. It was time to close shop anyway, because Gold Star, the crown jewel of sixties recording, was not completely keeping up with the times. (Though Spector's last production there, The Ramones' *End of the Century* [1980] attested that the place could still be utilized in the right hands.) After a fire in 1984, the building was knocked down, and a mini-mall built. It's a shame they didn't save some of the original bricks—in an era when paintings are fetching millions, pieces of "the wall of sound" could probably command a hefty price.

THE GOLDEN APPLE
7711 Melrose Avenue
West Hollywood

Melrose is not exactly a rock and roll street, though rockers shop here. It first gained notoriety in the late 1970s when punk-rockers hung out in its stores and clubs, but by the mid-1980s it evolved into what it is today, a stylish stretch of clothing and accoutrements shops. The Golden Apple is a comic-book/pop culture emporium with a rock and roll slant. They stock rock books (particularly 50s and 60s stuff) alongside their extensive comic book and pop culture stock. When Axl Rose of Guns N' Roses wanted to get a tattoo of Vampirella made, he came here to get the comic book, and rockers like Rob Zombie and members of many other bands shop here. In addition, Brooklyn-born owner Bill Liebowitz can tell you virtually anything you want to know about doo-wop, and if prodded, he'll demonstrate his yo-yo skills.

GOLDEN GATE THEATER
Atlantic Blvd. & Whittier Blvd.
East Los Angeles

This old theater, which has presented most of East L.A.'s most famous bands—Julian Herrera, Thee Midniters, Cannibal and The Headhunters, The Jaguars, and so many others—stands right in the heart of East L.A., at the intersection of its two most famous streets. The song "Whittier Boulevard" by Thee Midniters was a clarion call for cruisers back in the 1960s, and Whittier Boulevard was packed every Saturday night with "low riders," cars that are fixed up and lowered so they ride close to the ground. For the teenagers of East L.A., Saturday night cruising on Whittier Boulevard was the summit of the week's social activity. (The practice of cruising continued here into the 1980s, but was eventually stopped by the police and the community.) The cover of Rhino's *Best of Thee Midniters* shows the band hoisting Little Willie G on their shoulders in front of the Golden Gate Theater.

JIM GORDON MURDER SITE
6540 Havenhurst
Van Nuys

(Do Not Disturb Occupants) Jim Gordon was one of the two or three best rock drummers in L.A. throughout the 1960s and 1970s, both in concerts and on recordings (Traffic, Zappa, George Harrison, many others) and he was a member of Derek & The Dominoes (it's him playing piano at the end of "Layla"). But his mental state deteriorated in the 1980s and session work grew scarcer as he seemed to pay more attention to voices in his head than those around him. On the night of June 3, 1983 the voices told him to kill his mother, which he did somewhere in this condo complex. In 1984 Gordon began serving a sentence at the California Men's Colony in San Luis Obispo that will stretch well into the next century. (That facility also housed Ike Turner in the early 1990s.)

GREEK THEATER
Griffith Park
Los Feliz

A beautiful, outdoor theater at the south entrance to Griffith Park that serves as a venue for pop music. Over the years Joni Mitchell, Crosby, Stills and Nash, X, The Band, and Rickie Lee Jones have graced its stage. And who can forget Neil Diamond's 1972 *Hot August Night* album which was recorded here? Especially popular shows inspire "tree people" who climb the hills behind the arena and sit precariously on tree limbs, risking their lives for art, or at least for a free show. (When parking there, beware of "stacked" parking, in which nobody leaves until everyone does—a must to avoid.)

GRIFFITH OBSERVATORY
Griffith Park
Los Feliz

Famed for James Dean's scenes in *Rebel Without A Cause* shot here (they've even erected a statue of him here—strange for a facility to honor the actor whose character disrupted a lecture and got into a knife fight, but this is a strange town), the observatory is also used for album covers and video shoots: The Byrds' *Untitled* (1970) album is one; The Church's *Gold Fix Afternoon* (1990) album is another. Also, Laserium runs here as an independent adjunct to the observatory. Their shows, which feature rock and classical music in interplay with laser lights, and which now show all over the world, originated here in 1973.

GUITAR CENTER
7425 Sunset Blvd.
Hollywood

Erected on the site of the old Oriental movie house, this guitar shop has carried on a Hollywood-like tradition in laying down its own Walk of Fame, rock and roll style. Eddie Van Halen, Les Paul, Frank Zappa, Greg Allman, Little Richard, Stevie Wonder (they sell keyboards too), and dozens of others are enshrined with their handprints on the sidewalk in front of the store. The surrounding area is a guitar ghetto, rife with guitar shops.

GUNS N' ROSES FORMER APARTMENT
1114 N. Clark
Hollywood
(Do Not Disturb Occupants)

Members of Guns N' Roses lived here intermittently with manager Vicky Hamilton for more than a year in the early 1980s when they were first getting started. The apartment is only a couple of feet from The Whisky. This area has always been a hotbed of rock and roll housing: Nikki Sixx of Mötley Crüe and Blackie Lawless of WASP were roommates near here, and Joan Jett had her first apartment just down the street (See JOAN JETT).

CORNELL GUNTER GRAVE
Inglewood Park Cemetery
720 East Florence Avenue
Inglewood

Los Angeles native Cornell (Cornelius) Gunter sang tenor on such Coasters hits as "Charlie Brown," "Yakkety Yak," and "Poison Ivy." He grew up in a musical household—in 1954 his sister, Shirley, scored a rhythm and blues hit, "Oop Shoop," with her group Shirley Gunter and The Queens. (Platters singer Zola Taylor is often identified as Gunter's sister, but this is untrue.) Gunter started singing professionally with The Flairs, a group which included Richard Berry (See LOUIE LOUIE BIRTHPLACE), and then joined The Coasters in 1957. He left in 1961, but resurfaced later in the decade with Cornell Gunter and The Coasters, one of many Coasters splinter groups to follow. Gunter's Coasters were set to perform in Las Vegas, when, on February 27, 1990, he was shot on a street in North Las Vegas in what police called a random killing.

THE HARD ROCK CAFE
(former location)
300 E. 5th
Downtown Los Angeles

Back in 1969, when photographer Henry Diltz shot this storefront for the back cover of The Doors' *Morrison Hotel* album, this was Skid Row. The neighborhood's gotten worse.

THE HARD ROCK CAFE
Beverly & San Vicente
West Hollywood

In the northwest corner of the behemoth Beverly Center, this place was the first of what is now a chain of restaurants featuring "rock and roll" ambiance. Its walls adorned with famous people's guitars and memorabilia, it became a well-known "brat-pack" watering hole around 1987, and still draws tourists and natives alike. The angled Cadillac on the roof was inspired by The Cadillac Ranch art piece outside Amarillo, Texas. This Hard Rock had to purchase the name from the decrepit Hard Rock Cafe pictured on the back of The Doors' *Morrison Hotel* album (see previous entry).

TIM HARDIN DEATH SITE
625 North Orange
Hollywood

Tim Hardin was a West Coast singer/songwriter (born in Eugene, Oregon, December 23, 1941) who made his name on the East Coast in the mid-1960s, penning "If I Were a Carpenter," a hit when recorded by Bobby Darin (ironically, Hardin's only chart record as a singer, "Simple Song of Freedom" (1969), was written by Darin) and "Reason to Believe," recorded by, among other people, Rod Stewart. (Trivia note: See the incomplete graffiti, "Tim Hardin is a..." on the wall behind the band on the back of the *Do You Believe in Magic* album.) Hardin's soft-spoken songs belied his alcohol and heroin addictions—Jim Morrison once took Danny Sugerman to see Hardin to show him the ravages of hard drugs (See CHATEAU MARMONT)—and in 1970 Hardin moved to England to take advantage of the country's liberal methadone program. Though he told friends he was off drugs when he took this Hollywood apartment late in 1980, he died here December 29, 1980 of an overdose.

HARMONY PARK

(former location)
1514 Broadway
Anaheim

This old dance hall was once filled to bursting with kids jammed in to hear Dick Dale, "King of the Surf Guitar." Back in 1961, Dale's brand of loud, reverb-laden rock instrumentals blazed a trail for a string of imitators. (At the same time, The Belairs were mining similar ground in Redondo Beach. See BEL AIR CLUB.) Dale didn't start his surf music here. In 1961 he began playing at the Rendezvous Ballroom (now burned own) in Costa Mesa, across the street from a record store and electronics repair shop he owned. That summer, Dale developed a guitar-playing style—loud, clamorous, and with plenty of reverb (effected by putting the switch on his Fender Stratocaster between the settings)—that would revolutionize the sound of music in California and the world. (When he was in the Air Force stationed in San Pedro, Jimi Hendrix would beat a path to The Rendezvous to see Dick Dale whose left-handed guitar playing he admired.) In 1963, when Dale landed a recording contract with Capitol Records, he didn't stray too far from home, preferring to play here at Harmony Park Fridays and Sundays to overflow crowds. But despite a promising career that included an appearance in Muscle Beach Party, he didn't have the staying power of The Beach Boys. When his musical career faded, he invested in real estate and lay low. Currently he lives in the desert, plays occasional gigs and makes movie appearances, including *Back to the Beach.* In the 1980s, the old Harmony Park housed Peppertree Faire, a swap meet for antiques and crafts. Vendors sold their wares right at the stagefront where people once shoved tight to get close to Dick Dale. It was torn down in 1993.

WYNONIE HARRIS GRAVE

Woodlawn Cemetery
Central & Greenleaf

Wynonie "Mr. Blues" Harris was the king of rhythm & blues in post-war America. A handsome man with stunning stage movements and a gravelly, booming voice (Elvis Presley was greatly influenced by him), his version of "Good Rockin' Tonight" was the definitive one and his recording of "Bloodshot Eyes" became an anthem for the Jump (sometimes mistakenly called "swing") movement of the 90s. So is his grave marked with a monument the size of, oh, the Lincoln Memorial? Sorry. Wynonie must've spent all his money on good living, because he's interred here in an unmarked grave with three others, stacked. At least he got respect when he was alive.

HAUNTED HOUSE
(former location)
6315 Hollywood Blvd.
Hollywood

A teen nightclub of the mid-1960s, the scenes from *It's A Bikini World* were filmed here with performances by the Animals, Castaways, Toys, and Pat & Lolly Vega. Also used in the film *The Girl In The Gold Boots*. It was described in the Frank Zappa "freak map" as "fulla go-go & snappy ensembles & hairdos & a genuine firebreathing bandstand."

(SOME) HIGH SCHOOLS AND THEIR ROCK AND ROLL ALUMNI

ANAHEIM
Bobby Hatfield (Righteous Brothers)

ANTELOPE VALLEY
Frank Zappa
Don Van Vliet (Captain Beefheart)

ARCADIA
Stevie Nicks
Michael Anthony (Van Halen)
John Vidican (Kaleidoscope)
Bassett (La Puente)
Kid Congo Powers (Cramps, Gun Club)

BELMONT
Sonny Knight ("Confidential" 1956)
Mike Stoller (of Leiber and Stoller)
Marvin Phillips (Marvin and Johnny, "Cherry Pie")

BEVERLY HILLS
Jimmy Greenspoon (Three Dog Night)
Maria McKee (Lone Justice)

BIRMINGHAM
Bobby Sherman
The Jacksons

CANOGA PARK
Jay Ferguson (Spirit, Jo Jo Gunne)
Mark Andes (Spirit, Firefall)
Centennial (Inglewood)
Charles Fizer (Olympics)
Melvin King (Olympics)

Hollywood High School

Eddie Lewis (Olympics)
Walter Ward (Olympics)

CLEVELAND (VAN NUYS)
Pamela Des Barres (GTOs)
Victor Hayden (Captain Beefheart)

COLTON
Jim Messina (Poco, Loggins and Messina)

CRESCENTA VALLEY (GLENDALE)
Syd Straw
Greg Sowders (Long Ryders)

DORSEY
Mike Love (Beach Boys)
Kendall Jones (Fishbone)

DOWNEY
Bill Bateman (Blasters)
James Hetfield (Metallica)
Karen and Richard Carpenter

EL CAMINO REAL
Angelo Moore (Fishbone)
Walt Kibby II (Fishbone)

EL MONTE
Country Joe McDonald
El Rancho (Pico Rivera)
Jeanette Jurado (Expose)

FAIRFAX
P.F. Sloan
Phil Spector
Carol Connors (Teddy Bears)
Marshall Leib (Teddy Bears)
Herb Alpert
Jerry Leiber (Leiber and Stoller)
Tracii Guns (L.A. Guns)
Anthony Kiedis (Red Hot Chili Peppers)
Flea (Red Hot Chili Peppers)
Hillel Slovak (Red Hot Chili Peppers)
Slash (Guns N' Roses)
Bryan MacLean (Love)

Fairfax High School

FONTANA
Sammy Hagar (Van Halen)

FREMONT
Darlene Love (Blossoms, Bob B. Soxx)
Gloria Jones (Blossoms)
Fanita James (Blossoms)
Randy Jones (Penguins)

GARFIELD
Cesar Rosas (Los Lobos)
Conrad Lozano (Los Lobos)
David Hidalgo (Los Lobos)
Louie Perez (Los Lobos)

GRANT
Jeff, Steve and Mike Porcaro (Toto)
Steve Lukather (Toto)
Micky Dolenz (Monkees)
Jim Gordon (Derek and the Dominos)

Stan Lee (Dickies)
Tom Scott (L.A. Express)
Hamilton (Culver City)
Chris Dowd (Fishbone)
Norwood Fisher (Fishbone)
Fish (Fishbone)

HAWTHORNE
Brian Wilson (Beach Boys)
Dennis Wilson (Beach Boys)
Emmit Rhodes (Merry Go Round)

HOLLYWOOD
Ricky Nelson
Johnny Crawford ("Cindy's Birthday," 1962)
Lowell George (Little Feat)

IMMACULATE HEART
Charlotte Caffey (Go-Go's)
Natalie Cole

INGLEWOOD
Sonny Bono
Don Murray (Turtles)

JEFFERSON
Jesse Belvin ("Guess Who")
Richard Berry (writer of "Louie Louie")
Cornell Gunter (Coasters)
Shirley Gunter ("Oop Shoop" 1954)

JORDAN
Brenda Holloway

LA CANADA
Chris Holmes (Wasp)

LOYOLA
Roddy Bottum (Faith No More)
Billy Gould (Faith No More)

MANUAL ARTS
Bobby Sheen (Bobb B. Soxx)
H. B. Barnum (record producer)
Marina (Huntington Beach)
Bob Forrest (Thelonius Monster)

MARSHALL
Michelle Phillips (Mamas and the Papas)
Mira Costa (Manhattan Beach)
Keith Morris (Black Flag, Circle Jerks)

MONROE
Jeffrey Lee Pierce (Gun Club)

MONTCLAIR
Cher

MUIR (PASADENA)
David Lee Roth

NEWBERRY PARK
Belinda Carlisle (Go-Go's)

NORTH HOLLYWOOD
Don and Dick Addrissi (writers, "Never My Love")
Julius Wechter (Baja Marimba Band)
Ruben Guevara (Ruben and the Jets)
Notre Dame (Van Nuys)
Danny Hutton (Three Dog Night)
Jerry Yester (Lovin' Spoonful)
Oakwood (North Hollywood)
Sam Phipps (Oingo Boingo)

PACIFIC PALISADES
Ron and Russell Mael (Sparks)
Susanna Hoffs (Bangles)

PACOIMA JR. HIGH
Ritchie Valens

PASADENA
Eddie Van Halen
Alex Van Halen
Pius X (Southgate)
Phil Alvin (Blasters)
Dave Alvin (Blasters)
John Bazz (Blasters)

POLYTECHNIC
Hadda Brooks
Sonny Criss
Hampton Hawes
Big Jay McNeely

"ROCK AND ROLL HIGH SCHOOL"
The setting for the 1979 movie featuring the
Ramones was a condemned high school off the
Harbor Freeway. Interiors were shot at Van
Nuys High School.

ROLLING HILLS (PALOS VERDES)
Debbie Peterson (Bangles)
Vikke Peterson (Bangles)

ROOSEVELT (BOYLE HEIGHTS)
Lou Adler

SANTA ANA
Bill Medley (Righteous Brothers)

SANTA MONICA (SITE OF REBEL WITHOUT A CAUSE)
Dick and DeeDee ("The Mountain's High" 1962)
Ry Cooder

STONEY POINT (CHATSWORTH)
John Frusciante (Red Hot Chili Peppers)
Sunny Hills (Fullerton)
Jackson Browne

TAFT
Jane Wiedlin (Go-Go's)
Joan (Larkin) Jett
Cherie Currie (Runaways)
Jackie (Fuchs) Fox (Runaways)
Holly Vincent (Holly and the Italians)
Steve Bartek (Oingo Boingo)

TROY (FULLERTON)
Mike Ness (Social Distortion)
Dennis Dannell (Social Distortion)
Casey Royer (Adolescents)

UNI (UNIVERSITY)
Jan Berry (Jan and Dean)
Dean Torrence (Jan and Dean)
Arnie Ginsburg (Jan and Arnie)
Nancy Sinatra
Randy Newman
Kim Fowley (record producer)
Tone-Loc
Carol Conners
Darby Crash (Germs)
Danny Elfman (Oingo Boingo)
Leon Schneiderman (Oingo Boingo)
Steve Wynn (Dream Syndicate)
John Densmore (Doors)
Robby Krieger (Doors)
Bruce Johnson (Beach Boys)
Sandy Nelson ("Teen Beat" 1959)
David Cassidy

VAN NUYS
Paula Abdul
Berton Averre (The Knack)

WESTCHESTER
Howard Kaylan (Turtles)
Mark Volman (Turtles)

HIGHLAND GROUNDS
742 N. Highland Ave.
Hollywood

A definitive nineties venue (it opened Jan 1, 1990), this quaint restaurant/beer & wine bar/coffee-house features acoustic performers of all stripes: folkies, hicks, glam bands, whatever. For instance: Beck and Lisa Loeb; Chuck E. Weiss held a weekly slot here for a couple of years; and Randy California did his last performance here. Owner Rich Brenner is proud of the club's "strong sense of community" — and who can argue with that?

HOLLYWOOD & ARGYLE
Hollywood

This grievously nondescript corner is unimportant save for it supplying a name for a group of Hollywood session men who recorded "Alley Oop" in 1960 — The Hollywood Argyles. ("Teen Beat" drummer Sandy Nelson remembers whooping, not exactly singing, in the background.) "Alley Oop" producer Gary Paxton ("Flip" of Skip & Flip) relocated to Nashville, where he has been involved with gospel music for many years.

HOLLYWOOD BOULEVARD WALK OF FAME
Hollywood

Established later than you'd think, in 1960, the "Star Walk" started with a few rock stars, but they were slow to add more until the 1980s, when they started awarding them to old-timers like Chuck Berry and Jerry Lee Lewis.

Following are the locations of some musicians' stars:

- **Benny Goodman**, 6101 Hollywood Blvd.
- **Jack Jones**, 6104 Hollywood Blvd.
- **Louis Jourdan***, 6153 Hollywood Blvd.
- **Paul Whiteman**, 6157 Hollywood Blvd.
- **Kate Smith**, 6157 Hollywood Blvd.
- **Johnnie Ray**, 6201 Hollywood Blvd.
- **Red Foley**, 6225 Hollywood Blvd.
- **Barry Manilow**, 6233 Hollywood Blvd.
- **Rosemary Clooney**, 6235 Hollywood Blvd.
- **Celia Cruz,** 6240 Hollywood Blvd.
- **Eddie Fisher**, 6241 Hollywood Blvd.
- **Lena Horne**, 6250 Hollywood Blvd.

- **Sammy Davis, Jr.**, 6254 Hollywood Blvd.
- **Doris Day**, 6278 Hollywood Blvd.
- **Fred Waring**, 6300 Hollywood Blvd.
- **Les Baxter**, 6314 Hollywood Blvd.
- **Peggy Lee**, 6319 Hollywood Blvd.
- **Tab Hunter**, 6320 Hollywood Blvd.
- **Johnny Cash**, 6320 Hollywood Blvd.
- **Rosemary Clooney**, 6325 Hollywood Blvd.
- **Tony Martin**, 6331 Hollywood Blvd.
- **Jim Lowe**, 6333 Hollywood Blvd.
- **Gene Austin**, 6332 Hollywood Blvd.
- **Stan Kenton**, 6349 Hollywood Blvd.
- **Bill Haley**, 6350 Hollywood Blvd.
- **Buck Owens**, 6350 Hollywood Blvd.
- **Pointer Sisters**, 6363 Hollywood Blvd.
- **Errol Garner**, 6363 Hollywood Blvd.
- **Robert Goulet**, 6368 Hollywood Blvd.
- **Alan Freed**, 6381 Hollywood Blvd.
- **Gene Autry**, 6384 Hollywood Blvd.
- **Vicki Carr**, 6385 Hollywood Blvd.
- **Tony Orlando**, 6385 Hollywood Blvd.
- **Frankie Laine**, 6385 Hollywood Blvd.
- **Hank Williams**, 6400 Hollywood Blvd.
- **Count Basie**, 6400 Hollywood Blvd.
- **Johnny Maddox**, 6401 Hollywood Blvd.
- **Georgia Gibbs**, 6404 Hollywood Blvd.
- **Tex Williams**, 6412 Hollywood Blvd.
- **Clyde McCoy**, 6426 Hollywood Blvd.
- **Yma Sumac**, 6445 Hollywood Blvd.
- **Jimmy Dorsey**, 6505 Hollywood Blvd.
- **Joe Williams**, 6508 Hollywood Blvd.
- **Phil Harris**, 6508 Hollywood Blvd.
- **Count Basie**, 6508 Hollywood Blvd.
- **Liberace**, 6527 Hollywood Blvd.
- **Duke Ellington**, 6535 Hollywood Blvd.
- **Sammy Cahn**, 6540 Hollywood Blvd.
- **Jose Feliciano**, 6541 Hollywood Blvd.
- **Nancy Wilson**, 6541 Hollywood Blvd.
- **Fleetwood Mac**, 6608 Hollywood Blvd.
- **Tom Jones**, 6608 Hollywood Blvd.
- **Lawrence Welk**, 6613 Hollywood Blvd.
- **Fats Domino**, 6616 Hollywood Blvd.
- **Joni James**, 6630 Hollywood Blvd.
- **Sonny James**, 6630 Hollywood Blvd.
- **Perry Como**, 6631 Hollywood Blvd.
- **Jerry Lee Lewis**, 6631 Hollywood Blvd.
- **Jerry Lewis**, 6631 Hollywood Blvd.
- **Tex Ritter**, 6631 Hollywood Blvd.
- **Billy Eckstine**, 6638, Hollywood Blvd.
- **Crosby, Stills & Nash**, 6666 Hollywood Blvd.
- **Marty Robbins**, 6666 Hollywood Blvd.
- **Guy Lombardo**, 6666 Hollywood Blvd.
- **Kenny Rogers**, 6666 Hollywood Blvd.
- **Andy Williams**, 6667 Hollywood Blvd.
- **The Monkees**, 6675 Hollywood Blvd.
- **Ferlin Husky**, 6675 Hollywood Blvd.
- **Tommy Dorsey**, 6675 Hollywood Blvd.
- **Harry James**, 6683 Hollywood Blvd.
- **Diana Ross**, 6712 Hollywood Blvd.
- **Scatman Crothers**, 6712 Hollywood Blvd.
- **Dolly Parton**, 6712 Hollywood Blvd.
- **The Spinners**, 6723 Hollywood Blvd.
- **Nelson Riddle**, 6724 Hollywood Blvd.
- **Ritchie Valens**, 6733 Hollywood Blvd.
- **Ella Fitzgerald**, 6738 Hollywood Blvd.
- **Rev. James Cleveland**, 6742 Hollywood Blvd.
- **Bing Crosby**, 6751 Hollywood Blvd.
- **Patti Page**, 6760 Hollywood Blvd.
- **Judy Garland**, 6764 Hollywood Blvd.
- **Sammy Kaye**, 6767 Hollywood Blvd.
- **Eddy Arnold**, 6776 Hollywood Blvd.
- **Ray Charles**, 6777 Hollywood Blvd.
- **Elvis Presley**, 6777 Hollywood Blvd.
- **Spade Cooley**, 6802 Hollywood Blvd.
- **Joni James**, 6814 Hollywood Blvd.
- **Billy Daniels**, 6819 Hollywood Blvd.
- **Peter Frampton**, 6819 Hollywood Blvd.
- **Henry Mancini**, 6821 Hollywood Blvd.
- **Annette Funicello**, 6834 Hollywood Blvd.
- **Thelonious Monk**, 6834 Hollywood Blvd.
- **Andrews Sisters**, 6834 Hollywood Blvd.
- **Pee Wee Hunt**, 6838 Hollywood Blvd.
- **Little Richard**, 6840 Hollywood Blvd.
- **Mahalia Jackson**, 6840 Hollywood Blvd.
- **Paul Anka**, 6840 Hollywood Blvd.
- **Roy Clark**, 6840 Hollywood Blvd.
- **The Bee Gees**, 6845 Hollywood Blvd.
- **Sons of the Pioneers**, 6845 Hollywood Blvd.
- **Dinah Shore**, 6901 Hollywood Blvd.
- **Wayne Newton**, 6909 Hollywood Blvd.
- **Glenn Miller**, 6915 Hollywood Blvd
- **Elton John**, 6915 Hollywood Blvd.
- **Olivia Newton-John**, 6915 Hollywood Blvd.
- **Bobby Vinton**, 6916 Hollywood Blvd.
- **Aretha Franklin**, 6920 Hollywood Blvd.
- **Tennessee Ernie Ford**, 6922 Hollywood Blvd.
- **Dionne Warwick**, 6922 Hollywood Blvd.
- **Bette Midler**, 6922 Hollywood Blvd.
- **Glen Campbell**, 6925 Hollywood Blvd.
- **Lefty Frizzell**, 6927 Hollywood Blvd.
- **Michael Jackson**, 6927 Hollywood Blvd.
- **Herb Alpert**, 6929 Hollywood Blvd.
- **Mickey Gilley**, 6930 Hollywood Blvd.
- **Lou Rawls**, 6931 Hollywood Blvd.
- **The Carpenters**, 6931 Hollywood Blvd.
- **Paul Williams**, 6931 Hollywood Blvd.
- **Tito Puente**, 6933 Hollywood Blvd.
- **Nat King Cole**, 6959 Hollywood Blvd.

- **The Everly Brothers**, 7000 Hollywood Blvd.
- **Patti Labelle**, 7000 Hollywood Blvd.
- **Julie London**, 7000 Hollywood Blvd.
- **Donna Summer**, 7000 Hollywood Blvd.
- **Berry Gordy**, 7000 Hollywood Blvd.
- **5th Dimension**, 7000 Hollywood Blvd.
- **Engelbert Humperdinck**, 7000 Hollywood Blvd.
- **Mills Brothers**, 7000 Hollywood Blvd.
- **Lionel Hampton**, 7000 Hollywood Blvd.
- **Julio Iglesias**, 7000 Hollywood Blvd.
- **Guy Mitchell**, 7000 Hollywood Blvd.
- **David Bowie**, 7021 Hollywood Blvd.
- **Gloria Estefan**, 7021 Hollywood Blvd.
- **Paula Abdul**, 7021 Hollywood Blvd.
- **Anita Baker**, 7021 Hollywood Blvd.
- **Frankie Lymon**, 7033 Hollywood Blvd.
- **Stevie Wonder**, 7050 Hollywood Blvd.
- **Sam Cooke**, 7051 Hollywood Blvd.
- **The Beatles**, 7051 Hollywood Blvd.
- **George Benson**, 7055 Hollywood Blvd.
- **Herbie Hancock**, 7057 Hollywood Blvd.
- **Supremes**, 7060 Hollywood Blvd.
- **Della Reese**, 7060 Hollywood Blvd.
- **4 Tops**, 7060 Hollywood Blvd.
- **Temptations**, 7060 Hollywood Blvd.
- **Pearl Bailey**, 7080 Hollywood Blvd.
- **Don Cornelius**, 7080 Hollywood Blvd.
- **Benny Carter**, 7080 Hollywood Blvd.
- **Leiber & Stoller**, 7083 Hollywood Blvd.
- **Elmer Bernstein**, 7083 Hollywood Blvd.
- **Gladys Knight**, 7083 Hollywood Blvd.
- **Irving Berlin**, 7095 Hollywood Blvd.
- **Smokey Robinson**, 1500 Vine
- **The Jacksons**, 1500 Vine
- **The Beach Boys**, 1500 Vine
- **Janet Jackson**, 1500 Vine
- **Quincy Jones**, 1500 Vine
- **Rick Nelson**, 1500 Vine
- **Marvin Gaye**, 1500 Vine
- **Xavier Cugat**, 1500 Vine
- **Neil Sedaka**, 1500 Vine
- **Spike Jones**, 1500 Vine
- **Johnny Mathis**, 1501 Vine
- **Rod McKuen**, 1501 Vine
- **Percy Faith**, 1501 Vine
- **James Brown**, 1501 Vine
- **Clive Davis**, 1501 Vine
- **Carl Smith**, 1517 Vine
- **Gale Storm**, 1519 Vine
- **Perez Prado**, 1529 Vine
- **Billie Holliday**, 1540 Vine
- **Les Paul and Mary Ford**, 1541 Vine
- **Mel Tormé**, 1541 Vine
- **Roy Acuff**, 1541 Vine
- **Steve Lawrence & Eydie Gorme**, 1541 Vine
- **Tony Bennett**, 1560 Vine
- **Tommy Sands**, 1560 Vine
- **Webb Pierce**, 1600 Vine
- **Vaughan Monroe**, 1600 Vine
- **Xavier Cugat**, 1601 Vine
- **Dean Martin**, 1617 Vine
- **Jo Stafford**, 1625 Vine
- **Pat Boone**, 1631 Vine
- **Frank Sinatra**, 1637 Vine
- **Nelson Eddy**, 1639 Vine
- **Al Hibbler**, 1650 Vine
- **Jimmy Wakely**, 1680 Vine
- **Maria Callas**, 1680 Vine
- **Artie Shaw**, 1701 Vine
- **Teresa Brewer**, 1708 Vine
- **Slim Whitman**, 1709 Vine
- **Dave Brubeck**, 1716 Vine
- **Kay Starr**, 1716 Vine
- **Al Jolson**, 1716 Vine
- **Chuck Berry**, 1717 Vine
- **Hoagy Carmichael**, 1720 Vine
- **Dick Haymes**, 1724 Vine
- **Ella Mae Morse**, 1724 Vine
- **Sarah Vaughan**, 1724 Vine
- **Vic Damone**, 1731 Vine
- **Bobby Darin**, 1735 Vine
- **John Lennon**, 1750 Vine
- **Tina Turner**, 1750 Vine
- **Bob Seger**, 1750 Vine
- **The Steve Miller Band**, 1750 Vine
- **Gene Vincent**, 1751 Vine
- **Buddy DeSylva**, 1750 Vine
- **Anne Murray**, 1750 Vine
- **Helen Reddy**, 1750 Vine
- **Natalie Cole**, 1750 Vine
- **Garth Brooks**, 1750 Vine
- **Roy Anthony**, 1751 Vine
- **Ethel Merman**, 1751 Vine
- **Ernest Tubb**, 1751 Vine
- **Duran Duran**, 1770 Vine
- **Billy Vera**, 1770 Vine
- **Chuck Berry**, 1777 Vine

Though the frenchman who sang in Gigi made records, his musical significance pales next to 1940s R&B recording genius Louis Jordan (no "u"), who was undoubtedly the intended recipient of this star.

THE HOLLYWOOD BOWL
2301 N. Highland Ave.
Hollywood
Built in 1929, it's seen the best rock acts, from the 1960 Dick Clark/Art Laboe show with Frankie Avalon, Freddy Cannon, et al., to The Beatles, Bob Dylan, Donovan, Santana, Elton John, Janis Joplin and many others. Hendrix opened for The Monkees here in 1967. A Doors performance was recorded live here in 1968 and released on video. This beautiful outdoor arena seats 18,000. Today, it concentrates mainly on classical music, as well as on an annual jazz festival. (As with the Greek Theater, beware of "stacked parking" in the lot.)

THE HOLLYWOOD HAWAIIAN HOTEL
(former location)
Yucca & Grace
Hollywood
These rooms held a lot of musicians. In his 1977 song "Desperadoes Under the Eaves," Warren Zevon sings about sitting here listening to the air conditioner hum. Joe Selvin's book, *Ricky Nelson: Idol for a Generation,* recounts Ricky and songwriter Sharon Sheeley go-

ing to the Hollywood Hawaiian in 1958 to pick up The Everly Brothers, who were staying there. (It all ties in—before going solo, Zevon played piano with The Everly Brothers.) Pink Floyd stayed here in the late sixties, as did The Kinks. In 1970, when Jeremy Spencer of Fleetwood Mac left to mail a letter and never came back, he left from this hotel.

HOLLYWOOD PACIFIC BUILDING
6425 Hollywood Blvd.
Hollywood
In the early 1960s, this place held the offices of Sam Cooke's SAR Records and Lew Chudd's Imperial Records until Imperial's sale to Liberty in 1963 and Cooke's death in 1964.

THE HOLLYWOOD PALLADIUM
6215 Sunset Blvd.
Hollywood

Opened in 1940, this 5000-capacity (not seated) venue has been host to a giant selection of music, from Frank Sinatra in the forties, to The Teenage Fair in the early sixties, to The Rolling Stones, The Grateful Dead, The Who, David Bowie, The Ramones, The Clash, the 1973 Surf Revival, Chuck Berry (the 1973 concert where he kicked Keith Richard off the stage, discussed in the Chuck Berry bio-movie Hail Hail Rock and Roll), the Blues Brothers movie concert scene, the Grammy awards, Mexican dances...everything. In photos of the Palladium from the sixties and seventies you see Lawrence Welk's name atop the marquee, as he owned the place and broadcast his TV show from here.

HOLLYWOOD ROOSEVELT HOTEL
7000 Hollywood Blvd.
Hollywood

Opened with great fanfare in 1927 (the first Academy Awards ceremony was held here), this place grew shaky by the 1970s, but in the mid-1980s underwent a tremendous overhaul that made it one of the first "magnet" buildings of the "New Hollywood." The attached Cinegrill restaurant/nightclub has been presenting cabaret acts since its reopening in 1987. Some rock stars stay here, and The Everly Brothers are said to be investors, which could account for their Walk of Fame star being right on this corner. Also famed for a once-only punk show featuring The Go-Gos, The Germs, The Mau-Maus and Hal Negro & The Satintones.

HOLLYWOOD SIGN
Mt. Lee
Hollywood Hills

Erected in 1923 for the Hollywoodland housing development, it's smiled down on Hollywood ever since. (Occasionally it didn't smile, like when an unsuccessful actor or actress would try to use it as a permanent ticket out of show business.) The sign fell into decrepitude in the 1970s, and demolition was considered until a group of Hollywood do-gooders donated $27,000 each for its restoration in 1978. Musical contributors were Alice Cooper, who donated the last "O" on behalf of his friend Groucho Marx, and crooner Andy Williams, who donated the "W."

THE HOLLYWOOD SUNSET MOTEL

(former location)
8300 Sunset Blvd.
West Hollywood.

When Bob Dylan played The Hollywood Bowl in 1965, he stayed here, as did Al Kooper. It is now a retirement home called the Golden Crest Hotel.

HOUSE OF BLUES

8439 Sunset Blvd.
West Hollywood

Since it opened in late 1994, this club has not just dominated the upper end of the L.A. club scene, it has become it. High priced club acts (Tom Jones), auditorium fillers (Eric Clapton), local bands (the Sprague Bros.) and more all play this 1100-capacity instant-landmark, leaving all other clubs behind. Owned overtly by Dan Ackroyd and supported by a cabal of Hollywood high-rollers who pay to keep the blues alive (blues acts do play here, there's a gospel lunch every Sunday, and they sponsor workshops in Watts), it must be saluted for filling this city's need for a large nightclub with a blues/roots emphasis. Of course there are those who complain that the club with such a name is not an 'authentic' Mississippi Blues Shack (though part of it is), but most people simply shrug like Joe E. Brown in *Some Like It Hot* and say "Nobody's perfect!" Don't miss the spectacular Elvis Presley Birthday Bash held here every January 8th.

HOUSE OF FREBERG LIMITED (BUT NOT VERY)

(former location)
89720 Sunset
West Hollywood

Satirist Stan Freberg had his headquarters here during the 1960s, producing ads and occasional music parodies. The humorist grew up in Pasadena and cut all his great Capitol records in Hollywood. His monumental *Stan Freberg Presents the History of the United States of America* was released in 1990 on CD with extra cuts. Volume 2 of this record was released in 1996 and was a runaway hit for Rhino Records. This building was once a Hollywood designer's studio and now houses a fancy restaurant.

THE ICE HOUSE
24 North Mentor
Pasadena

The popular folk club of the fifties, sixties and seventies is now a comedy club (with music thrown in too), still nestled down an alleyway off Colorado Blvd. People who've played here include Peter Tork (pre-Monkees), Roy Brown, Steve Martin, The Association, The Standells, Bob Lind, Ian Whitcomb, Hearts and Flowers, The Yellow Balloon and many other folk, country and blues-oriented acts.

BILLY IDOL CRASH SITE
Gordon & Fountain
Hollywood

February 6, 1990, Billy Idol, celebrating both the completion of his new album, Charmed Life, and the imminent arrival of his parents from England, took an 8 a.m. spin on his motorcycle. For no apparent reason he spilled the bike at this intersection and suffered a broken arm and broken leg.

IRV'S BURGERS
8289 Sunset
West Hollywood

This was the location for the inner foldout of Linda Ronstadt's *Living in the U.S.A.* (1978). The same photo could not be taken today because the garage next door has erected a fence.

THE IVAR THEATER
1605 Ivar
Hollywood

Recently a strip-show house, The Ivar was a legit theater when Lord Buckley recorded a live album there on February 12, 1959, and when The Grateful Dead played there on February 25, 1966. (The Tom Waits song, "Emotional Weather Report," makes reference to "a ticket taker's smile" at The Ivar.) Strip shows have only recently ceased.

JACK'S SUGAR SHACK
1707 Vine St.
Hollywood

After a couple of years bouncing around various locations in the early 1990s, Jack settled his tropical decor club here, a few feet from Hollywood & Vine. Roots-rock and country and blues are always on tap. Don't miss Ronnie Mack's long-lived widely-loved Barn Dance here Tuesday nights — it's free, and jammed with stars both known and not.

BILLY JAMES
FORMER RESIDENCE
8404 Kirkwood
Laurel Canyon
(Do Not Disturb Occupants)

When Columbia A&R man Billy James moved to Elektra Records in 1967, he moved into this Laurel Canyon home. His house was a gathering place for musicians, including Jackson Browne, who lived downstairs in the laundry room for about a year. (James, when at Columbia, wrote the liner notes to the first Byrds album, and signed The Doors—whose option Columbia later dropped due to lack of interest.) From 1969 to 1971, James also co-owned The Black Rabbit Inn at 8727 Melrose, a mellow show-biz boîte that was partly bankrolled by Elmer Bernstein, Jack Nicholson and The Doors, among others.

JOAN JETT FORMER RESIDENCE
1025 San Vicente Blvd.
West Hollywood
(Do Not Disturb Occupants)

Rocker Joan Jett lived in this apartment in 1977, when she first moved to Hollywood. Not surprisingly, it is close to The Whisky (it would be in the club's shadow if the sun shone from the north). Jett began her musical career in the all-girl hard rock group The Runaways in 1975. In 1978 she produced the first Germs album. She began her own band, Joan Jett and The Blackhearts in 1979, through an ad in Music Connection magazine. Their fame grew steadily, from small gigs around L.A. to international success in 1982 with "I Love Rock & Roll".

BENNY JONES'S HOUSE

(former location)
3438 W. 118th Pl.
Inglewood

In early 1962, musician Gary Usher ("Driven Insane", Titan, 1960) came to visit his uncle Benny at his house on the Inglewood/Hawthorne border. Like everyone for several square blocks, he heard rock & roll blasting from the Wilson family garage on nearby 119th St., and walked over to see what was going on. He struck up a friendship with the band, The Beach Boys, then collaborated with bandleader Brian, writing two of the Beach Boys' biggest hits, "409" and "In My Room." Usher went on to create studio bands like the Hondells and the Super Stocks, produced three Byrds' albums (*Younger Than Yesterday, Sweetheart Of The Rodeo, Notorious Byrd Bros.*), and become head of A&R for RCA Records, among other things. He died May 25, 1990 of lung cancer at age 51

JANIS JOPLIN DEATH SITE

Landmark Hotel
(now the Highland Gardens)
7047 Franklin Ave.
Hollywood

Once Janis Joplin took the stage at The Monterey Pop Festival in 1967 she was on a one-way rocket to the top— only to die alone at age twenty-seven, in room 105 of this Hollywood hotel from an overdose of heroin. A lot has been written about the pain Joplin endured. Roundly rejected in her hometown of Port Arthur, Texas (she was voted "Ugliest Man on Campus" in a college poll) in 1966 she fled to San Francisco to seek a new life, and found it with the band Big Brother and The Holding Company. They grew with San Francisco's burgeoning music scene, and she was catapulted to the top, becoming the single most celebrated singer of that town and that era. Wealth, fame and world acclaim followed, yet she remained the wild, sad, hippie girl with a pint of Southern Comfort always at hand. Her death here at the Landmark Hotel on October 3, 1970 from an overdose of pure heroin (reportedly mistaken for diluted) was a shock to fans throughout the world. Her latest album *Pearl* (1971), had shown a new maturity that seemed to promise even better days. "Me and Bobby McGee" from that album was her first number one hit, averring "freedom's just another word for nothing left to lose."

JOSHUA TREE NATIONAL FOREST
Cap Rock
Joshua Tree
When Gram Parsons' body (See GRAM PARSONS DEATH SITE) disappeared from the L.A. airport September 20, 1973, police suspected devil-worship or worse, but the reason for the theft was friendship. Depressed at band-mate Clarence White's funeral a few weeks earlier, Parsons told road manager Phil Kaufman that he didn't want a funeral if he died, he wanted his body to be burned in the desert. Kaufman, and partner Michael Martin, took the body from the airport (where it was to be flown to New Orleans for burial) in a hearse (which made their ruse believable to airport authorities) and drove to Cap Rock in Joshua Tree. (Kaufman says Cap Rock was not a favorite spot of Parsons, it was chosen because they were too drunk to drive any further and afforded ample getaway space.) They doused Parson's body in gasoline and lit it, causing at first a fireball, then bubbling and "melting" of the body. The perpetrators fled, and the remains were once again routed to New Orleans where they were buried.

JUMBO'S CLOWN ROOM
5153 Hollywood Blvd.
Hollywood
This is the strip club where Courtney Love allegedly danced topless when she first moved to L.A.

PHIL KAUFMAN FORMER RESIDENCE
Chandler St, W. of Ethel
North Hollywood
(Do Not Disturb Occupants)
After the arrest of road manager Phil Kaufman, and partner Michael Martin, for stealing Gram Parsons' body from the airport and immolating it at Cap Rock (See JOSHUA TREE NATIONAL FOREST), a concert was held in the back yard here to raise money

for him. (The criminal charge was reduced to misdemeanor theft, and settled with a fine). Barry Hansen, radio's Dr. Demento, remembers that there was a small crowd for Kaufman's Koffin Kaper Koncert, with acts ranging from Barry 'Boris' Pickett ("Monster Mash") to The Modern Lovers. The show raised a few bucks for Kaufman (rodeo tailor "Nudie" Cohen dropped by and donated $500), and he resumed his career as, to cop the title of his autobiography, a Road Mangler Deluxe. Among the more noted residents of Kaufman's guest house were Gram Parsons and various members of the Manson family (before their "notoriety"). But perhaps Kaufman's attitude was encapsulated best on his personalized license plate which read PH KAUF (someone took offense and the DMV revoked it.)

JOHN KAY
FORMER RESIDENCE
7408 Fountain
Hollywood

Steppenwolf founder John Kay moved into this small apartment above a garage in June, 1967, after the breakup of his band Sparrow. (Sparrow had come to LA from their native Toronto in November 1966 to play It's Boss, then fled town after the December 1966 Sunset Strip Riots [See PANDORA'S BOX] made club bookings scarce.) He got together with next-door neighbor Gabriel Mekler to cut some demos with his new band Steppenwolf. Songs were rehearsed and polished in the garage, leading to the band signing to ABC—Dunhill and Mekler producing, among others, "Born To Be Wild" and "Magic Carpet Ride."

KENNEDY HALL
451 S. Atlantic Blvd.
East Los Angeles

One of the big concert venues in the 1960s where major deejays like Art Laboe and Huggy Boy would run shows mixing national and local acts that appealed to the Mexican-American community. The shows would usually sell out and disappointed kids would spread onto local streets and alleys and often get into trouble. Cesar Rosas of Los Lobos happily remembers hanging outside the Kennedy Hall every weekend with his homeboys when he was a teenager—a memory he shares with many other people from this part of town.

CAROLE KING FORMER RESIDENCE
8815 Appian Way
Laurel Canyon
(Do Not Disturb Occupants)

Carole King bought this house when she moved to L.A. from New York in the late 1960s. Here, in November 1970, photographer Jim McCrary snapped her picture for the cover of *Tapestry*. During the sixties, King, along with then-husband Gerry Goffin, penned hits including "Up on the Roof," "Will You Love Me Tomorrow," "The Locomotion," and "You Make Me Feel Like a Natural Woman." Though she was primarily a songwriter, King also had a hit record in 1962 with "It Might As Well Rain Until September." Moving to L.A. after the breakup of her marriage, she enjoyed modest success with her first solo album, *Carole King: Writer* (1970) and then *Tapestry* (1971) went through the roof, ultimately selling thirteen million copies—then the biggest-selling album in the history of the record business. *Tapestry* was the high-water mark for Ode Records, the label founded by longtime L.A. music figure Lou Adler. Adler's credits include producing Jan and Dean, founding Dunhill Records, and producing Barry McGuire ("Eve of Destruction") and The Mamas and The Papas, organizing The Monterey Pop Festival in 1967, and founding Ode, whose acts besides King included Scott McKenzie ("San Francisco [Be Sure To Wear Flowers in Your Hair]") and Spirit ("I Got a Line On You").

KMET
(former location)
5828 Wilshire Blvd.
Los Angeles

Los Angeles' rich radio history is recorded in other books, but this one bears special mention for its powerful effect on L.A. In the early 1970s "FM Rock" swept America with disjointed (well, joints were involved), free-form radio that made radio-listening an adventure and a joy. Begun in December 1971, KMET featured a roster of deejays that included Dr. Demento, Jim Ladd, Steven Clean, Mary Turner, Jeff Gonzer, Shadoe Stevens, and Jimmy Rabbit. (Rabbitt's evening show freely mixed Hank Williams and Waylon Jennings with ELO and other current rock music, not-insignificantly contributing to the growth of country music in pop circles at that time. He was mentioned in a David Allen Coe song, had his own album on Capitol, and his grandfather was

Leon Payne, who wrote both "I Love You Because" and "Psycho.") Dr. Demento's 2-hour nationally-syndicated radio shows went on two extra hours in LA, until 1983, on KMET. The station jingle was sung by The Persuasions. It closed officially in 1987, but was really on its way out in 1977. It is still missed.

KNICKERBOCKER HOTEL
1714 Ivar
Hollywood

This venerable old hotel, in the heart of Hollywood, housed Elvis Presley and The Jordanaires during the summer of 1956, when Presley was here recording the Elvis album and filming *Love Me Tender*. Jerry Lee Lewis also had a suite here at the height of his popularity, early in 1958.

LA CIENEGA & SUNSET
West Hollywood

It's frustrating to imagine this strip of small businesses at this corner in, say, 1966, when local bands played the Sea Witch Nightclub here, or in 1955 when Specialty Records had its offices at 8608, or the twenty-plus years when Dino's Lodge was the western end of this row, as all are torn down and the space built anew.

LAS PALMAS THEATER
1642 Las Palmas
Hollywood

Known seemingly for centuries as a major/minor theatrical venue, it debuted *The New Faces of 1952* revue which included Eartha Kitt, Ronny Graham, Paul Lynde, and Carol Lawrence, and in the mid 1980s was the first home for Jackie Mason's incredibly successful *The World According To Me*. But its inclusion in this book is for Sly Stone's scheduled November 13, 1987 show, for which he didn't show up. Maybe that was smart of him, for it not only fulfilled some expectations (he was the most famous no-show in rock history - riots sometimes followed his absences) but it also delayed his following night's arrest in front of the theater.

LATE FOR THE SKY COVER SITE

215 S. Lucerne, Hollywood
(Do Not Disturb Occupants)

Photographer Bob Seidemann snapped the front of this house in 1981 for the cover of the Jackson Browne album.

LAUREL CANYON COUNTRY STORE

2108 Laurel Canyon Blvd.
Laurel Canyon

The place "where the creatures meet" in The Doors "Love Street." When Glen Frey of The Eagles first came to L.A. in the early 1970s, the first celebrity he saw was David Crosby, shopping at this store.

LEMON GROVE PARK

Hobart & Lemongrove
Hollywood

In November, 1974, 20-year-old Tulsans Dwight Twilley, Phil Seymour, and Bill Pitcock IV moved to L.A. to become rock stars. Within two weeks they signed to Shelter Records, ex-Tulsan Leon Russell's label. Just before Thanksgiving, and prior to a scheduled trip to Tulsa for demo sessions, Twilley walked to this park and

wrote "I'm On Fire." In Tulsa, rather than make demos they worked solely on "I'm On Fire," and the resultant record, released in April, 1975, shot to #16 nationwide. Looking back, band members said "We didn't know it was supposed to be hard to get a record deal and a hit." Twilley, now living in Tulsa, continues recording. Seymour, after a solo career and a stint with the Textones in the 1980s, died August 17, 1993 of lymphoma.

LEWIN'S RECORD PARADISE
6507 Hollywood Blvd.
Hollywood.

Lewin's was THE place to get British imports in the early, exciting mid-1960s— they seemed to have a pipeline from London to Hollywood. As time passed and tastes changed, it is said to have continued its au courantness by specializing in live-performance bootleg albums. Folklore maintains that they escaped hassles by suppyling rock stars with their own bootlegs gratis. (In his book, One Is The Loneliest Number, former Three Dog Night man Jimmie Greenspoon glowingly describes the importance of Record Paradise to kids in LA in the mid-1960s.)

LIBERTY RECORDS
(former location)
1560 La Brea
Los Angeles

This L.A. based company started in the mid-1950s, hitting with Julie London and Patience and Prudence, and then with Martin Denny, Eddie Cochran, Jan and Dean and The Chipmunks. (Chipmunks creator David Seville named his characters after the label's three founders: Simon Waronker, Alvin Bennet and Theodore Keep.) United Artists

Records, which absorbed Liberty in the early seventies, had hits with Kenny Rogers, War and ELO; and then EMI, which swallowed UA, operated here until 1989. (Trivia note: in the late 1970s, UA record labels were printed on a colorful orange sky that symbolized "Sunset" and "Orange," their street intersection.) Today the property is on the block and will probably make one heck of a shopping center.

THE LIDO APARTMENTS
Yucca & Wilcox
Hollywood

The lobby of the Lido was used for the interior shots on the Eagles' Hotel California album.

LINDA'S DOLL HUT

107 S. Adams
Anaheim

This club has proved to be Orange County's, and maybe LA's, most formidable roots and new-rock club despite its holding, officially, only 49 people. Linda Jemison (at first with an ex-partner ex-husband) transformed the local bar into a musician-friendly music venue starting in 1989 (previously, The Pontiac Brothers had used the club's name and facade on an album cover). Among the acts who've played here over the years: Social Distortion, Offspring, Laika & The Cosmonauts, Los Straitjackets and nearly every roots-rock band, local or otherwise.

LITTLE RICHARD 1959 HOME

1710 Virginia Road
Los Angeles

(Do Not Disturb Occupants)
Little Richard was responsible for breaking the color barrier in popular music. Until his arrival on the scene in 1956, popular black records were commonly "covered" by white groups for popular consumption. But Little Richard's records were too wild and too unique for this—white record buyers weren't satisfied with the Pat Boone version of "Tutti Frutti," they clamored for Little Richard's original. He rode the crest of that fame, through "Long Tall Sally," "Jenny, Jenny," "Rip It Up," "Lucille," and many more, to hair-raising appearances in the films *The Girl Can't Help It* and *Don't Knock the Rock*. In late 1957, Little Richard was truly on top of the world, in a plane flying to Australia, when an engine caught fire, and he made a vow: If he survived that flight he would give up rock and roll and dedicate his life to the Lord. The plane made it, and the Lord got him. From then until his comeback to the secular world in 1962, Little Richard renounced his rockin' ways and preached wherever people would listen. Before renouncing everything, he bought his mother this elegant house, in which he was married(!) in 1959 to Ernestine Campbell. (The marriage didn't last.) Little Richard has endured, surviving a near-fatal auto accident in 1985, making a series of comebacks, including a new career as an actor in "Miami Vice" and *Down and Out in Beverly Hills*.

"LOUIE LOUIE" BIRTHPLACE
142 W. 54th Street
Los Angeles
(Do Not Disturb Occupants)

In this quiet home rhythm and blues singer Richard Berry wrote "Louie Louie." Berry was a formative L.A. rock and roll musician. He was a founding member of The Flaires. He sang lead on The Coasters' "Riot in Cell Block Number Nine." His 1955 song "Next Time" was recorded by Louis Prima and Sam Butera. And he was "Henry" on Etta James' "Roll With Me, Henry." He wrote "Louie Louie" in 1955 and recorded it in 1956. In 1963, the song became controversial when recorded by The Kingsmen. Their version slurred the lyrics and people concluded they must be dirty. Teenagers eagerly made up dirty lyrics. (Sample: "I put my nose in her hair" for Berry's simple "I smelled the rose in her hair.") After investigation by no less than the FBI, the record was dubbed "unintelligible" and the controversy ended. Richard Berry died in 1994 and is interred at Inglewood Cemetery.

"THE LUCKY BUILDING"
8255 Sunset Blvd.
West Hollywood

Russ Regan, the record-exec who suggested The Pendletons change their name to The Beach Boys, calls this "the lucky building" because so many music businesses started here. It was the site of World Pacific jazz label (producer Nik Venet noticed a strong odor of wacko-tobacco here in 1960 when he produced The Moondawgs rock instrumental, "LSD-25"); A&M Records made their home here early on; two companies Regan headed, Uni and 20th Century, took flight from here; and Casablanca Records started out here in 1974 (moving one building west when they grew).

LUCY'S EL ADOBE RESTAURANT
5536 Melrose Ave.
Hollywood

This longtime watering hole for the film world—it's right across from Paramount Studios—became Southern California Rock Headquarters in the late 1970s when every Elektra/Asylum act on the roster, it seemed, hung out here. The Eagles, J.D. Southern, Andrew Gold–the whole lot, hung their eight-by-tens on the wall and partied beneath them. Linda Ronstadt reigned as Queen Bee, both for her artistry and her relationship with then-California governor Jerry Brown. They came here frequently together. Today it's still a well-attended eatery and the eight-by-tens remain.

MADAME WONG'S WEST

2900 Wilshire Blvd.
West Los Angeles

In 1977, when the punk movement was exploding, L.A's Chinatown became a new focus of musical energy. It started when entrepreneur Paul Greenstein persuaded Madame Wong's Chinese restaurant to open its doors to live music, and the nearby Hong Kong Restaurant followed suit. (The idea of having bands in after a restaurant closed was a popular one then. In San Francisco, the Philippino restaurant Mabuhay Gardens provided the same arrangement.) Bands of all persuasions and their fans flocked to Chinatown to see any of hundreds of new wave acts that were cropping up: Fear, The Heaters, The Knack, The Busboys, The Police, The B-52s. Buoyed by its success, Esther Wong opened a second Madame Wong's in Santa Monica. The wave collapsed in the mid-1980s when the Chinatown clubs closed, leaving only Madame Wong's West to carry on the rock band tradition which it did energetically until it closed in the early 1990s. It has now been replaced by a video store.

MACARTHUR PARK

Alvarado & Wilshire
Los Angeles

In 1968 Jimmy Webb wrote a perplexing song ("melting in the dark"? "there's a cake out in the rain"?) about this place and it rose to number two nationally. Richard Harris sang it. Some scenes from Nicolas Roeg's *The Man Who Fell to Earth* with David Bowie were filmed in is park. MacArthur Park still has playgrounds, foot-pedal boats and concerts, but it's a dangerous place at night, and a little dodgy in the daytime too.

MARTONI'S

1523 Cahuenga
Hollywood

A longtime watering hole for record company promotion men (the guys who get records played on the radio). Sonny Bono was a new star when he was denied entry here in 1965. His duet with his wife Cher, "I Got You Babe," was a smash, but his stardom was overshadowed by his looks. Sonny and Cher, in their wild mod get-ups (long hair, striped bell-bottoms, fur vest), caused such a stir at Martoni's that they were asked to leave along with their pal Rodney Bingenheimer. Hurt by this rebuff, Sonny wrote and recorded "Laugh at Me," which shot in to the top ten a month later. Sonny's pain at this rejection was probably keener than most peoples. He was thirty years old at the time and only a fringe member of the record community (he had co-written "Needles and Pins," a minor hit for Jackie DeShannon and later a large hit for The Searchers, and "She Said, Yeah," a non-hit for Larry Williams that was covered by The Rolling Stones) for more than a decade before succeeding in tandem with Cher. For him to make it big and still be ignored must have been a bitter pill to swallow. (Years later, when a feisty reporter asked him if he'd admit someone wearing a fur vest and striped bellbottoms to his new restaurant, Sonny laughed and didn't answer.) Martoni's closed in 1994.

THE MASQUE
(former location)
alley, Cherokee south of Hollywood Blvd.
Hollywood

This dank, spacious cellar beneath the former Pussycat Theater (now a Spanish language church), reachable through several secret entrances, was once the Masque, L.A.'s premiere punk-rock venue. When the Whisky and the Starwood wouldn't book "Thrash" acts like The Skulls, The Bags, The Weirdos and The Controllers, Scottish-born Mancunian-turned-Angeleno Brendan Mullen presented them here. The Masque opened July 1, 1977 and word spread fast. More bands came, including X, The Screamers and The Germs and the club did turn away business. Of course it attracted the attention of the police and fire marshals as well. After repeated warnings for operating without permits, inadequate fire exits and the like, the club was closed in January 1978, but remained in business as a rehearsal hall, crash pad and homeless shelter. It was finally closed in October 1979 by the cops and fire marshalls.

THE OTHER MASQUE
(former location)
6314 Santa Monica Blvd.
Hollywood

When the original Masque Club was prohibited from having live acts any longer, founder Brendan Mullen formed a partnership with Slash Records' Bob Biggs and they opened a second Masque in December 1978. It booked new local acts like The Plugz and The Go-Gos, and out-of-towners like The Cramps, The Dead Boys and Levi and the Rockats. But once again, under threat from the fire marshall, the second Masque closed late in February 1979. Mullen then turned to concert promoting, using little-known venues like the Ukranian Hall and the Stardust and presenting new bands like The Adolescents and Black Flag, until the big clubs saw the light and started booking these bands themselves. His reputation reestablished, in 1982 Mullen became the booker at Club Lingerie. (A Masque reunion in 1995 was broadcast on MTV.)

MASTER RECORDERS

(former location)
535 North Fairfax
Hollywood

Where they now sell kids clothes, recordings were made in the late 1950s. Among the records cut when this space housed Master Recorders: "Framed" by The Robins, "Searching'" by The Coasters, "She's Got It" and "Ooh! My Soul" by Little Richard, "Short Fat Fannie" by Larry Williams, and Ricky Nelson's "I'm Walkin'," "Hello Mary Lou" and "Lonesome Town"—in fact, every hit Nelson had during the first five years of his career.

PERCY MAYFIELD GRAVE

Inglewood Park Cemetery
720 E. Florence
Inglewood

Percy Mayfield was the king of the blues in 1950, a smooth-voiced, incredibly handsome man whose "Please Send Me Someone to Love" is still much-recorded and performed. His command of romantic blues made him a sepia sensation—his moody songs included such titles as "Two Years of Torture," "The River's Invitation," and "This Time You Suffer Too." A traffic accident in 1952 altered his looks and his career, which took a downslide, but he came back in the 1960s as a songwriter for Ray Charles, penning "Hit the Road Jack," "Danger Zone," and several others. Mayfield died at age sixty-three and was buried here August 17, 1984.

MCA RECORDS

100 Universal Plaza
Universal City

One branch of an entertainment giant so big it calls itself a city, MCA Records started in 1973 when the movie company bought Decca Records and inherited hit artists like The Who and Elton John. During the 1980s they acquired ABC-Dunhill, Chess and Motown Records and discovered and developed new talent like Tom Petty, Bobby Brown, Nanci Griffith and Lyle Lovett. Today their roster includes Erykah Badu, Trisha Yearwood, Mary J. Blige and The Mavericks.

MCCABE'S GUITAR SHOP
3101 Pico Blvd.
Santa Monica

The primary folk-music venue in L.A. (and the only one since the Ash Grove closed—See ASH GROVE) for twenty plus years, this venue also sells guitars, books, batik and organic cookies—a little island of Vermont in a hectic city. (During the early seventies the club was booked by Bobby Kimmel of The Stone Poneys.) Guy Clark, Doc Watson, Dave Van Ronk, Gibson and Camp, Bill Monroe, Sun Ra, John Lee Hooker, Clifton Chenier, Billy Bragg, Joni Mitchell, Joe Ely, and Don Cherry have played here, as have countless other folk, blues and jazz acts (and let's not forget the night in 1987 when Elvis Costello, Jackson Browne, Warren Zevon, and Richard Thompson played for former booker Nancy Covey's going-away party). Local rock musicians like Dream Syndicate, Firehose and Thelonius Monster have done acoustic music sets here, and R.E.M. recorded an acoustic version of "The One I Love" here, released as a twelve-inch single.

MERCEDES-BENZ HOLLYWOOD
(former location)
Sunset & Wilcox
Hollywood

Biographer Jerry Hopkins, in his book *Elvis: The Final Years*, reports that Elvis Presley bought six Mercedes-Benzes for friends at this dealership early in 1970. The dealer has since moved to a fancier location (probably partly financed by Presley profits), then fled Hollywood in 1997.

MILLIE'S RESTAURANT
3524 Sunset Blvd.
Silverlake

Canter's was "the top freako watering hole" for musicians in the '60's, and now Millie's serves the same purpose for musicians and allied ne'er-do-wells. It is not only a local rock eatery, it's also an employment site for musicians where you're likely to encounter members of the Circle Jerks or Thelonius Monster slinging hash. The running joke is that to work here you must have been dropped by a major label.

MODERN RECORDS

(former location)
5810 South Normandie
Los Angeles

This was the last of several addresses for the L.A.-based blues labels Modern, Flair and RPM. L.A. became a major center for blues records during World War II, and the Bihari Brothers, who founded Modern Records in 1944, catered to that burgeoning market. Modern issued records by John Lee Hooker, Jesse Belvin, B.B. King, Pee Wee Crayton and Elmore James, and then in the 1950s turned to pop music with groups like the Teen Queens (in 1956 their "Eddie My Love" was covered by The Fontane Sisters and The Chordettes, but all versions sold equally). During the 1960s Modern Records issued soul music with the Kent label, then reverted to budget-reissue packaging on Crown and other allied labels (including The Tops label—See TOPS).

MONDRIAN HOTEL

8440 Sunset Blvd.
West Hollywood

Formerly painted in the style of the famous painter Piet Mondrian, this fashionable place seems to get a lot of record business trade—both from businessmen and rock stars. (The controversial rape charge against singer Al B. Sure stems from an incident alleged to have taken place here.) Remodeled in 1997, the hotel has become known as the "cool" place to stay and also known for its popular (and difficult to get in to) Sky Bar which has become a trendy, celebrity hang out.

MONTEBELLO BALLROOM

(former location)
10th & Whittier.
Montebello

A "shrine" for young Latinos during the sixties, this place featured a mix of Chicano and soul acts, including Little Julian, Ronnie and The Pomona Casuals, The Jaguars, and The Johnsons Three Plus One (later called The Brothers Johnson). It has been a popular dance hall since the 1920s.

MONTECITO HOTEL
(now Montecito Apartments)
6650 Franklin Ave.
Hollywood
Once a toney hotel and host to, among other people, Elvis Presley, Bob Dylan, The Band and Willy DeVille, the Montecito has been converted to apartments.

MONTROSE BOWL
Montrose
This eight-lane bowling alley is such a perfectly-preserved 50s beaut that it's used more for movie and corporate parties than public bowling. The reason for its inclusion here were three parties in 1989 hosted by reclusive producer Phil Spector. Quarters were stacked on the jukebox and pinball machines, the kitchen was open to all, but the party didn't officially start until the mysterious host swept in around 11 p.m. and held court with select kegglers. Spector himself didn't bowl, but on the lanes at various times were Gerry Goffin, Shadow Morton, Ike Turner and many other select invitees.

MORRISON & DENSMORE
Encino
An intersection in the Valley not connected to The Doors except by coincidence—Morrison was the band's lead singer, Densmore the drummer.

MORRISON HOTEL
1246 S. Hope St.
Downtown Los Angeles

Photographer Henry Diltz asked the owner's permission to photograph The Doors here for the *Morrison Hotel* album cover in 1969. When he didn't get permission, he had the band run in and did it anyway. The portion pictured on the album is to the left of the hotel entrance.

JIM MORRISON LAST RESIDENCE
8216 1/2 Norton
West Hollywood

In 1970 Pamela & Jim Morrison rented this apartment upstairs from Doors publicist Dianne Gardiner. A gal wrote a whole book about a floor session with Jim here, but Gardiner remembers other times, like watching Jim's poetry books fly onto the lawn, flung out in disgust when the words weren't coming, or the worshipful look on his face when Chuck Berry came calling here.

FERDINAND 'JELLYROLL' MORTON GRAVE
Calvary Cemetery
4201 Whittier
Los Angeles

'Jelly Roll' Morton was one of the most important early jazz musicians, a fiery pianist of the 1920s who combined ragtime, blues and marches with a ferocity (not unlike Jerry Lee Lewis's to come) that at first startled and then amazed the music world. Morton was flamboyant and boastful, qualities that drove away many potential sidemen, even ones who wanted to play with him. His Victor recordings from 1926 to 1928 capture him best.

MUSIC MACHINE
(former location)
12220 Pico Blvd.
Santa Monica

This venue has featured rock music from all strata through the 1980s, though with an admitted penchant for blues, rockabilly and roots music. On one hand they were open to new music, including, The Violent Femmes, The Lords of the New Church, Jane's Addition, and X, and on the other they eagerly presented Bo Diddley, Big Joe Turner, Los Lobos, The Paladins, Queen Ida, Robert Cray, Junior Wells, Buddy Guy, Albert Collins, Albert King Clifton Chenier, Flaco Jimenez, Ry Cooder and Otis Rush. After doing dismal business in the early 1990s, the site was turned into a wholesale electrical supplier.

MUSICIAN'S UNION LOCAL 47
817 Vine St.
Hollywood

The place where thousands of the top musicians in the world are registered and get jobs. The union's files trace the history of recorded music in Los Angeles and, therefore, the world. In the city's early years (of the 20th century, that is) black musicians belonged to a segregated union, Local 767, with offices at 17th & Central. When the 47 and 767 merged in 1953, it had some detrimental effects on the former 767 members, for now they competed with many many others musicians for jobs. Veterans from the pre-1953 days still meet annually in the Los Angeles Clef Club. Its concert hall is used for shows and parties and its practice rooms are rented out for reasonable rates to union members.

"MY SHARONA" BIRTHPLACE
Highland & Romaine
Hollywood

In June 1978 when this building was a rehearsal hall, Doug Fieger, Berton Averre, Prescott Niles and Bruce Gary worked out the song Fieger and Averre had just written, "My Sharona." Triumphant, frenzied appearances (primarily at the Troubadour, where Bruce Springsteen and Stephen Stills, among others, joined them onstage) and worshipful press coverage (upon their success the press changed its tune) ensued and the band signed to Capitol. Their $18,000 debut album became a multi-million seller, propelled by the song generated here. Location is now a lumber sales building.

VINCE NEIL CRASH SITE
Sapphire & Esplanade
Redondo Beach
Late afternoon on December 8, 1984, Motley Crue singer Vince Neil, high on success and intoxicants, slid his 1972 Ford Pantera sports car through the stop sign on Sapphire (entering the picture from the right) and turned left (towards our camera) at an excessive speed. This view is the one seen by the 18-year-old female passenger of the northbound Volkswagen that Neil's car, swerving crazily into the oncoming lane, hit head-on; she was brutally injured and spent 3 weeks in a coma. Neil came out unhurt, but his passenger Nicholas "Razzle" Dingley, the drummer for Finnish band Hanoi Rocks, was killed, ending both his life and his band's. (Neil eventually paid $2.6 million to the injured parties and relatives of the deceased, and did public service work against drunk-driving.)

RICKY NELSON CHILDHOOD HOME
1822 Camino Palmero
Hollywood
(Do Not Disturb Occupants)
The Nelson family resided here throughout the 1950s— Ozzie, Harriet, David and the irrepressible Ricky. The facade of this house was used at the opening of the "Ozzie and Harriet" TV show. Next door was the real Thornbury family (though it wasn't

headed by anyone like the actor who played the lawnmower-borrowing Thorny in the show, Don Defore). The Nelson kids grew up here, and graduated (well, David did) from nearby Hollywood High, from whence teenaged Ricky would bolt daily at 3:30 for Scrivner's Drive-In (See SCRIVNER'S) to hear the latest platters. When Ricky became a rock and roll heartthrob, this street became a crowded cruising spot, especially for teenage girls angling for a glimpse of Ricky. Harriet sold the house in 1976, after Ozzie's death, and moved to Laguna Beach, where the family had often spent its summers. Ricky died in a plane crash on New Year's Eve 1985. He is buried in Forest Lawn Cemetery in the Hollywood Hills.

SANDY NELSON CRASH SITE

Mulholland 3 turns west
of Dixie Canyon Rd.

At 3 p.m. on April 22, 1963,
Sandy Nelson, the most famous drummer in rock & roll,
was heading west on
Mulholland on his motorcycle
when he found himself nearly

head-on with a school bus.
(Among the school bus passen-
gers was 13-year-old Bonnie
Raitt.) His left arm scraped the
side of the bus and then his bike
slid under it and his right leg
wrapped around the bus's rear
tire: the sound he heard "like a
waterfall" was blood gushing
from his crushed knee. After
three weeks hospitalization gan-
grene set in the leg, and on May 12th it was amputated above the knee. By the time Nelson got
up and around again it was 1964 and another, beringed, drummer captured the record-buying
public, and Nelson, though he continued recording into the 1970s, never recaptured his pre-
crash popularity. In 1998 he was living comfortably outside Las Vegas, occasionally playing
piano in a neighborhood cigar store.

9000 SUNSET BUILDING

9000 Sunset Blvd.
Beverly Hills

This office building once was a hub of the music business. Managers, bookers, and producers huddled close—perhaps stimulated by the
fact that Billboard, the music biz weekly, also
had offices there. Onetime Beatles publicist
Derek Taylor operated a PR business out of here
in 1967, representing The Byrds, The Doors,
Captain Beefheart and The Beach Boys, among
others. And Jim Morrison, never the shrinking
violet, did a dance atop the low wall on the
building's roof for his film *Hwy.* 9000 Sunset
is still an office building, but not the music industry beehive it once was.

NORTY'S MUSIC CENTER
(former location)
436 N. Fairfax Ave.
Los Angeles

Throughout the 50s and 60s Norton Beckman & his wife Clarice ran a top 40 record store here. It was a beacon for kids in this Fairfax High neighborhood including Phil Spector, Herb Alpert, and part-time songwriting employees Jerry Leiber and Steve Barri. Employee Simon Rutberg bought the place in 1986 and made it Hatikvah Music, the L.A. center for Jewish music. (Feel free to ask him about his co-compiling the Jackie Wilson *Mr. Excitement* box set for Rhino.) THE place for Jewish music on either coast.

NUDIE'S RODEO TAILORS
5015 Lankershim
North Hollywood

"Nudie" Cohen, who got his nickname in New York when he made rhinestone-encrusted g-strings for strippers, was the tailor to movie and rock stars alike. John Wayne and Roy Rogers were customers and so were Elton John, John Lennon, Eric Clapton, George Harrison, Ricky Nelson—the list is endless. Cohen made

his two most important suits for musicians. In 1946, he made a white suit with musical notes on it for Hank Williams. The exposure Hank gave Nudie propelled him into the limelight. Then, in 1956, Colonel Tom Parker had Nudie design and make a $10,000 gold suit for Elvis Presley that pushed Nudie permanently into the public eye. Nudie was a character. He played the mandolin, and would liven up parties just by arriving in this silver-dollar-and-steer-horn-studded convertible, both he and his wife Bobbie dressed head to toe in his custom-designed rhinestone-covered western finery. When he died on May 9, 1984, the entertainment world lost one of its most colorful figures. Though his wife Bobbie ran the business for several years after Nudie's death, in 1995 she closed down and the site is now a discount furniture store.

OCEANWAY STUDIO (FORMERLY UNITED)
6050 Sunset Blvd.
Hollywood

Famed in the 1960s as the recording site of innumerable hit records ("Bridge Over Troubled Waters," nearly all the hits by the Beach Boys, Mamas & Papas, and many others), its popularity has continued into the 1990s. (In 1995, historic Phil Spector sessions were held here with Celine Dion.) L.A. scenemaker Rodney Bingenheimer remembers attending a Blondie recording session here in 1980 when a car came crashing through the studio wall. The driver, Jeffrey, had been arguing with his girlfriend and lost control of the car. The result was a song, "Suzy and Jeffrey," which appeared on the flipside of the Blondie single "The Tide Is High." (See also UNITED WESTERN).

OKI DOG
(former location)
Santa Monica & Vista
Hollywood

The "Home of the Oki Dog" (a flour tortilla wrapped around two hot dogs and filled with chili and cheese) was a thorn in the neighborhood's side because of its popularity among punk rockers during the early 1980s. The restaurant didn't discourage lolling by mohawked teenage boys wearing kilts, and managed to eke out a business until it closed in 1989, long after punk rock had crested. A famed Germs "live" LP ends with lead singer Darby Crash hollering, "Let's all go to Oki Dog!" This historical site now houses a Fatburger.

OLYMPIC AUDITORIUM
1801 South Grand
Downtown Los Angeles

L.A.'s longtime wresting venue was also host to rock and roll shows. During the 1950s the Olympic held some house-rocking rhythm and blues shows under the aegis of deejay Hunter Hancock. San Francisco promoter Bill Graham also ran it in the late 1960s as an L.A. alternative to the Fillmore. In the 1970s there was a memorable show in which Little Richard was joined onstage by too many revelers and the stage collapsed. During the 1980s it was best known for punk shows (what better place than a wrestling arena?!) with PiL, Fear, X, Motorhead, Black Flag and others. Fela Kuti and other African acts played here late in that decade, and parts of many movies are shot in its cavernous confines (including scenes for *The Doors*).

THE ONION
Sepulveda Unitarian
Universalist Society
9550 Haskell
Sepulveda

Long known as the onion dome church—today, officially, The Onion—this place was the Valley Unitarian Church in early February 1966, when the Grateful Dead played here as part of the Acid Test series. At this "happening," organized by San Francisco LSD-touters the Merry Pranksters, people danced to the music of the Dead and ate pineapple chili, while Neal Cassady, of Jack Kerouac's *On the Road* fame, and Hugh Romney, known henceforth as Wavy Gravy, egged them on. Other musicians played here too. In the mid-1970s, L.A. resident Ray Campi, "the king of rockabilly," did shows here that set the pace for his barnstorming tours of England and Europe that continue today. And in the late 1980s the church began jazz dinner shows which featured, among others, Buddy Collette and Wild Bill Davidson. The Onion has long been a haven for progressive thinkers. During the 1960s it was a hippie/radical centers where many war protests were staged, and today it remains an activist center, raising money for Salvadoran refugees and other causes. It is still available for rental any time except Sunday mornings when church services are held.

ROY ORBISON GRAVE

Pierce Brothers Cemetery
1218 Glendon
Westwood

Roy Orbison rose from humble origins to world fame—more than once. Born April 23, 1936 in Vernon, Texas, Orbison pursued music from an early age, forming a band in high school, and in 1956 (through Pat Boone, a classmate at North Texas State College) met Johnny Cash and got a recording deal with Sun Records. No hits ensued (though "Ooby Dooby" has since become a rockabilly classic, recorded by Creedence Clearwater Revival, among others) and Orbison turned to songwriting, penning "Claudette," a hit for the Everly Brothers. In 1959, he signed with the Nashville-based Monument label, and in 1960, his recording of "Only the Lonely" started him on a long run of hits, including "Oh, Pretty Woman," and the yearning ballads "Running Scared," "It's Over," "In Dreams," and "Crying." He toured American and Europe as a star in the early and mid-1960s, and numbered among his admirers Elvis Presley and the Beatles. But the 1960s were hell in Orbison's private life. His wife, Claudette, died in a motorcycle accident in 1966, and two year later two of his sons perished in a fire. By the late 1960s, shifting musical tastes pushed Orbison off the pop music charts and he stayed off them for nearly twenty years. (The exception was "That Loving You Feelin' Again," a 1980 duet with Emmylou Harris that topped the country charts and was also a minor pop hit.) In the late eighties Orbison made a dizzying return to the public eye. First, his song "In Dreams" was used as a centerpiece in the 1987 movie Blue Velvet; then he joined in a recording project with George Harrison, Tom Petty, Bob Dylan and Jeff Lynne called The Traveling Wilburys, which resulted in a hit tune, "Not Alone Anymore." And then, signed to Virgin Records, he scored a number one hit with "She's a Mystery to Me." Sadly, though, Orbison never got to see his music hit the top of the charges again. On December 6, 1988, he died of a heart attack in Henderson, Tennessee. He had lived with his second wife, Barbara, in Malibu for a year. Like Frank Zappa, his grave at Pierce Brothers Cemetery is unmarked by a headstone. Carl Wilson is also buried here.

ORIGINAL SOUND RECORDS

7120 Sunset Blvd.
Hollywood

Back in 1959, deejay Art Laboe was getting so many requests (See SCRIVNER'S) for old records that he issued an album of them, calling it *Oldies But Goodies* and inventing a field of music and a phrase that swept the world. Laboe's Original Sound Records was established to re-

lease 'oldies' but almost immediately began issuing new music: "Teen Beat" by Sandy Nelson and "Bongo Rock" by Preston Epps were hits in 1959, and later came "Talk Talk" by the Music Machine. Lesser known was "Grunion Run" by the Hollywood Persuaders, actually Paul Buff and Frank Zappa, whose "Memories Of El Monte" (harking back to Laboe's pioneering rock shows at the El Monte Legion Stadium – rock & roll was considered so explosive that the city of LA would not allow shows in the city limits) was recorded by the Penguins for Original Sound. In the late 1960s, Sugarloaf's "Green Eyed Lady" and the Strawberry Alarm Clock's "Incense and Peppermints" were recorded in the label's recording studio. In the middle 1970s, one of Original Sound's warehouse men, Barry White, broke big as a solo act – on another label. Today, *Oldies But Goodies* continue to sell worldwide, and Laboe is still signing new groups. (Don't show up here, send a tape. Not oldies.)

JOHNNY OTIS FORMER RESIDENCE
2077 S. Harvard
Los Angeles
(Do Not Disturb Occupants)
L.A. r&b pioneer Johnny Otis lived in this house from 1950 until well into the 1970s, raising a family — his best-known progeny, Shuggy (a variation on his affectionate - confectionate? - name, Sugar) was featured on the 1971 album Super Sessions 2 — and the roof when-

ever he played. Otis worked tirelessly to promote r&b music in the postwar years; his revues at the Barrelhouse on LA's booming Central Avenue were the launching pads for future stars including Etta James and Esther Phillips. But like so many pioneers he was bypassed when rock & roll sprouted from the seeds he helped plant: he had but one chart record, "Willie & The Hand Jive," in 1957, but he continued making music and presenting, and producing, soul musicians old and new via television, radio, and his own record label. In the 1980s he hosted a popular blues radio show over KPFK in L.A. Now living in the Napa Valley region of California, Otis remains a champion of black and mixed-race (born to Greek parents, he early on developed a Negro identity) music, whatever it's called.

"OUR HOUSE"
Lookout Mountain Rd.
Laurel Canyon
(Do Not Disturb Occupants)
This house is where Joni Mitchell lived when she wrote *Clouds* and *Ladies of the Canyon*. (The cover of the latter was sketched from the kitchen window view.) When Crosby, Stills and Nash first formed they practiced here. And when Graham Nash lived here with Joni, he wrote "Our House."

The house is now owned by Ron Stone of Gold Mountain Management, which handles Bonnie Raitt, Belinda Carlisle, Alannah Myles, The Allman Brothers and Pat Benatar.

THE PALACE
1735 Vine St.
Hollywood

Built back in 1927 as a legitimate theater, then used for television, this hall's first significant rock moment occurred in June 1964, when Dean Martin, hosting "The Hollywood Palace" TV show, went out of his way to insult his musical guests, The Rolling Stones. Typical of his disdain for the band was his remark, "Now don't go away anybody—you wouldn't want to leave me with these Rolling Stones, would you?" Surely the feeling was mutual. (One of the poems on the back of the *Another Side of Bob Dylan* album includes the line, "an dean martin should apologize t the rolling stones.") During the 1970s the Palace lay fallow, but it rebounded in the eighties as the peppy disco/concert theater we know today, featuring big-name rock acts that have included R.E.M., The Bangles, The Neville Brothers, The Fabulous Thunderbirds, The Stray Cats, The Cramps, The Blasters and on and on.

THE PALOMINO
6907 Lankershim
North Hollywood

The Palomino was Los Angeles' premier country music nightclub and in the 1980s extended its scope into other areas of music. Founded in 1949 by country singer Hank Penny (who took the club name from the collar of a cowboy shirt), The Palomino was sold to two brothers from Indiana, Tommy and Billy Thomas, in 1950 and proceeded to become one of the most important country music showcases in the world, booking Johnny Cash, Lefty Frizzell, Patsy Cline, Buck Owens, Merle Haggard, Linda Ronstandt, Waylon Jennings and countless others. During the 1980s, under scion Bill Tomas, The Palomino's focus became more diffuse. Elvis Costello played here with Ray Campi opening. Bob Dylan, George Harrison and John Fogerty jammed one night with Taj Mahal and Jesse Ed Davis. Jerry Lee Lewis used to fill the place, but so did The Paladins, Junkyard and The Red Hot Chili Peppers. Though it later lost the rough-and-tumble reputation it had in the fifties, the Pal is still probably best remembered for the night in 1976 when Tiny, the bouncer, got shot with an arrow by an angry patron he'd ejected. (Tiny quit soon afterward.) The front sidewalk contains one Hollywood Boulevard-like "star." In the late 1970s the club planned a Country Music Walk of Fame for itself, but couldn't get a city permit. The one star they laid down, Eddie Rabbitt's, remains. Unfortunately, the club shut down in 1994 and its future is still unknown.

PAN PACIFIC AUDITORIUM

(former location)
Beverly & Curson
Hollywood

Nothing is left of this once-fabulous art deco modern building that fell to ruin following a devastating fire in 1988. Built in 1935, the Pan Pacific was already on its last legs in 1957 when Elvis Presley played two shows here on October 28th and 29th. (Does anyone speak of his first L.A. show, June 8, 1956, at the Shrine Auditorium? It seems buried in history—See ELVIS PRESLEY L.A. CONCERTS.) All manner of Hollywood's youth—Ricky Nelson, Nick Adams and Tommy Sands were among the many that came out to see Elvis do a very short set (preceded by acrobats and jugglers) that was inaudible over the screams of teenage girls. After it was over, you heard, "Elvis has left the building" over the PA system. (At a party after the show, Elvis met Ricky Nelson and both were surprised to learn of the other's admiration.) A less pleasant memory of the Pan Pacific involves its use as a backdrop in the roller-disco movie *Xanadu* in 1980.

PANDORA'S BOX

(former location)
Sunset & Crescent Heights
Hollywood

When you ask about the Sunset Strip in the sixties, everyone says, "Pandora's Box," like a rallying cry. Why? Because the place was torn down right after the 1966 Sunset Strip disturbances (the location is now a bus stop). Buffalo Springfield's "For What It's Worth" was written about the fracas here—police drew a line and forbade people to cross it—but the part about paranoia running deep cut two ways. Pandora's Box, a small beatnik club (bongo player Preston Epps was the mainstay) from the 1950s, was changed into a teen nightclub in 1962 by deejay Jimmy O'Neill (who later hosted TV's "Shindig"). The Beach Boys played one month, but mostly it featured a house band which included Leon Russell and David Gates (later of Bread). In 1966, restless kids gathered around Pandora's Box nightly, and cops routinely rousted them for curfew violations. Confrontations ensued, and the cops won. (A picture in the L.A. Free Press at the time showed bail-bond information posted on the club's marquee. The Freep was located then in an office below the club.) Shortly after the mêlées, which spanned a couple of weeks, the club was closed and then torn down. Goddamn repressive paranoid overkill, right? Maybe not. The demolition of Pandora's Box was a long-held plan. O'Neill remembers the city's wanting to remove it in 1962 to straighten out a traffic-flow problem on Sunset. That the city chose to do so after the youth flare-ups could be coincidental. If so, there are a lot of people still carrying grudges for nothing. In any case, there is a traffic island where Pandora's Box once stood.

PARADISE COVE

North of Malibu

It looked like a cold day in 1962 when the newly-signed Beach Boys posed for their first album cover on this stretch of beach north of Malibu. This is one of the covers that features "comeback king" Beach Boy David Marks. This beach is a private one, with a gate charge for pedestrians or drivers. "Paradise Cove" was a local hit for the Surfmen, covered by The Lively Ones and Martin Denny. (The Sand Castle restaurant and adjoining parking lot was the site of James Garners' trailer in "The Rockford Files.")

THE PARK SUNSET HOTEL

8462 Sunset Blvd.
West Hollywood

Eddie Cochran wrote "Summertime Blues" while staying at this hotel in 1958. At the time, it was a hub for Cochran, his lawyer, Walter Hurst, his producer, Jerry Capehart, his pals Johnny and Dorsey Burnette and Baker Knight, writer of "Lonesome Town."

GRAM PARSONS DEATH SITE

(Joshua Tree Motel—now Copper Sand Youth Camp)
Route 62, Joshua Tree

Country-rock pioneer Gram Parsons died in room number 8 of the Joshua Tree Motel from a drug overdose on September 19, 1973. He was twenty-nine. Parson's star-crossed career took him from folk and country music roots in his native Florida (in a band with Jim Stafford and Kent "Lobo" Lavoie) to interna-

tional fame. His onetime girlfriend and collaborator Emmylou Harris' fame surpassed Gram's a few years after his death. In the mid-1960s Parsons moved to New York with a rock band. Then, after moving to L.A., he joined The Byrds as keyboard player and shaped that band's new country direction. Soon he formed his own country-oriented rock band, The Flying Burrito

Brothers, but that band failed to dent the charts, and he lay low for a couple of years, resurfacing as a solo performer in 1972. Parsons was a magnetic character who extolled the virtues of country music to a rock and roll world that only half listened. "His" Byrds album, *Sweetheart of the Rodeo*, was their worst seller, and The Burrito Brothers, too, fell into the crack between rock and country. He is said to have influenced The Rolling Stones, whose guitarist, Keith Richards, he was close to. Parsons' tragic death followed only by months the accidental death of former Byrd Clarence White, who was hit by a car after a gig in Palmdale, California (See CLARENCE WHITE). Controversial in life, Parsons was also controversial in death (See JOSHUA TREE NATIONAL FOREST).

LES PAUL'S FORMER RESIDENCE
1514 Curson
Hollywood
(there are no occupants)
It's the exception rather than the rule when the city of L.A. allows a building with musical significance to remain standing. Les Paul's house is no exception. In the late 1940s and early 1950s when guitar wizard Paul's house WAS here his garage was his tinkering shop and recording studio. (Besides being a hit record-maker with his wife Mary Ford, he helped develop multi-track recording and a rather popular guitar.) After a while it was so filled with amps and pre-amps and double-track and quadruple-bypass tape machines that the door was no longer a door and visitors had to squeeze in through an enlarged window. What remains of this fantastic shop, the guitarists' equivalent to Tom Edison's Menlo Park lab?—the lovely parking lot you see here (It's the LA motto — "No room for tribute, we gotta park.")

PEPPERMINT WEST
(former location)
1750 Cahuenga Blvd.
Hollywood
In 1963, this was a popular rock and roll dance club, where celebrities like Jayne Mansfield would come. Good dancers were paid five dollars a night to show up and inspire others. One day, producers of the Elvis Presley movie Viva Las Vegas corralled the best dancers to appear in that film's

productions numbers. The house band was The Standells, whose new dance, The Peppermint Beatle, never caught on. The club closed in the mid-sixties and the site, once occupied by a Volkswagen dealership, is now torn down.

PERKINS PALACE

(former location)
Holly & Raymond Streets
Pasadena

Frequently opened and closed, this old theater saw a slew of local-band concerts during the 1970s, and then, when heavy metal exploded in the early 1980s, started serving a steady diet of metallists including Ratt, Mötley Crüe, Armored Saint, Megadeth, Poison and more. Guns N' Roses established themselves as a major band after seven consecutive sold-out shows here in 1987.

PHIL'S DINER

11138 Chandler
North Hollywood

The album cover of Phil Everly's second solo album, *Phil's Diner,* was taken here in 1975. Today, the label that issued the album, Pye (U.S.) is out of business and so is Phil's Diner and Phil Everly has successfully rejoined his brother Don in The Everly Brothers.

ESTHER PHILLIPS GRAVE

Forest Lawn Hollywood Hills
Burbank

Born Esther May Jones on December 23, 1935, in Galveston, Texas, "Little Esther" was first discovered at age fourteen when, living in L.A. she won a talent contest at Johnny Otis' Barrelhouse Club on south Central Street. Recordings with modern, Federal and Savoy Records ensued. (Her Federal platter with The Dominoes, "The Deacon Moves In," a song in which she defends herself from the advances of a lecherous preacher, is one of the greatest records ever made.) Phillips continued to make records and appearances sporadically throughout the 1950s, and then scored a big hit with a haunting version of the country song "Release Me," which made it to number eight nationwide in 1962. During the 1970s she came into a different, more mature fame when she recorded jazz/blues for the Kudu label—few can forget Aretha Franklin's renunciation of a Grammy in 1975, saying Esther deserved it more. Drug and alcohol abuse slowed Phillips down in the early 1980s, and finally killed her. She died August 17, 1984, age forty-nine, of complications from liver and kidney ailments.

THE PHONE BOOTH
(former location)
Southwest corner, La Cienega &
Santa Monica Blvd.
West Hollywood

Now a Fatburger, the hamburger stand popularized by "Sanford and Son," and previously the site of the Great American Food and Beverage Company (where aspiring singers sang in diners' faces), during the late 1960s this was one location of the Phone Booth (another was across the street, on the northwest corner), a topless bar frequented by Jim Morrison, whose band's office was next door on Santa Monica.

PICO & SEPULVEDA
West Los Angeles

This was a nondescript corner in 1947 when Felix Figueroa (actually bandleader Freddy Martin) recorded "Pico and Sepulveda" for a joke—but the song spawned the career of radio personality Doctor Demento. Record archivist Barry Hansen played "Pico and Sepulveda" frequently on his fledgling "Demented Discs" show on KPPC-FM in Pasadena in 1970 (KPPC was the first successful "underground" rock station in L.A.) leading him, and his alter-ego Doctor Demento, to nationwide fame. Today, his syndicated radio show is heard in over 175 markets—due in no small part to the silly song written about this still nondescript intersection.

PINK'S
711 N. La Brea Ave.
Hollywood

Most non-vegetarian rockers have come to this hot dog stand to the great and near-great at least once. It's said that Phil Spector, after cutting a new hit at Gold Star recording studios, would pile his musicians into a car and take them to Pink's to celebrate.

PLUMMER PARK PARKING LOT
Fountain & Plummer
Hollywood

In 1966, this plot of land held the house of manager Barry Friedman, and was a home away from home for a new group consisting of Steve Stills, Richie Furay, Dewey Martin, Neil Young and Bruce Palmer. In early 1966, Fountain Avenue was being widened and someone pried the Buffalo-Springfield nameplate off of a road-grating machine and hung it on Friedman's living room wall. Visitor Van Dyke Parks (who was once set to be in the band) says he suggested they adopt this for their name, and the rest is history. (Parks' claim to naming the group is "the last word" on the subject because he's the last person I asked. In John Einarson's book about the band, co-written with Dewey Martin, it was Martin who had the idea. Actually, it's hard in LA to find someone who DIDN'T choose their name.)

POLLIWOG PARK
Beach & Redondo Blvd.
Manhattan Beach

Picnickers hurled food and insults at Black Flag during its debut performance at the bandshell here in 1978. The band had assured park officials that its music was "kinda like Fleetwood Mac."

ELVIS PRESLEY
BEVERLY HILLS HOMES
1960-1963 — 565 Perugia Way
1963 — 1059 Bellagio Road
1963-1965 — 565 Perugia Way
1965-1967 — 10550 Rocco Place
1967-1977 — 144 Monovale
(Do Not Disturb Occupants)

This beautiful house at 565 Perugia Way is where—wait! It's been torn down! Maybe to discourage Elvis fans. (A new house now occupies this site.) The house that formerly sat here, just up the street from the Bel Air Country Club, was where Elvis lived twice, and where he met the Beatles on the night of August 27 1965. (The Beatles were in town for a pair of shows at the Hollywood Bowl [See BEATLES RESIDENCE 1965]. Their meeting was uncomfortable—The Beatles were awed in his presence

and Elvis, it is said, didn't much like them or their music—but they managed to squeeze in a jam session during their three-hour visit.) Elvis' final home at 144 Monovale (not where he died—that was at Graceland in Memphis), was the home in which he lived the longest, and it isn't nearly as visible as this one. A high brick wall prevented onlookers from seeing anything but the tip of the roof.

Elvis Presley Los Angeles concerts

June 8, 1956 — Shrine Auditorium
October 28/29, 1957 — Pan Pacific Auditorium
November 14, 1970 — The Forum
November 14/15, 1972 — Long Beach Arena
April 23/24, 1973 — Anaheim Convention Center
May 11, 1974 — The Forum
April 25,1976 — Long Beach Arena
November 30, 1976 — Anaheim Convention Center

P.J. PROBY
FORMER RESIDENCE
880 Hilldale
West Hollywood

Sure, this isn't the same place rented by Jim Smith when he was Jett Powers (some name!), but it's the address used on his 1960 drivers license. Smith was a Hollywood Hopeful, emigrating from Texas in 1957 and landing minor film parts, making records that didn't sell, and hanging around with hard-living brothers Johnny and Dorsey Burnette. In 1964 he was discovered by British producer Jack Good, who whisked him to England and dubbed him P.J. Proby. There, dressed in ruffled shirts and a sporting a ponytail, he became a one-man American Invasion with hit records, tv appearances, and concerts. All seemed well for P.J. except for two things: his drinking, and a propensity for splitting his tight pants during shows. The British press and censors stood for the pants-splitting once or twice — they'd lightened up since banishing Jerry Lee Lewis in 1958 — but when the trouser-tears became chronic, the jig, and his career, were up: by 1965 he was persona non grata. (Just like Jim Morrison after wagging his weenie in Miami.) He settled in England: in 1979 he portrayed Elvis Presley in a long-running West End musical, and he still does occasional club dates.

PROFESSIONAL DRUM SHOP
854 Vine St.
Hollywood

Founded in 1959 by the late Bob Yeager (his wife still oversees the business, which is run by her two sons), Professional is now the only Los Angeles store devoted exclusively to drums and live (not electronic) drummers. Its walls are lined with new and fading pictures of skin-beaters of the past 40 years, its customers, inevitably, have included everyone in the biz, from neophyte Dennis Wilson, who wrote his first check here in 1961, to veteran session giant Hal Blaine (who can keep a mean beat but cannot, according to the photo here, get his socks to match).

RADIO RECORDERS RECORDING STUDIO
7000 Santa Monica Blvd.
Hollywood

Opened by Harry Bryant in 1936, it saw plenty of movie and music industry action (the latter before the major labels opened their own studios). Elvis recorded "Teddy Bear," "Jailhouse Rock," "All Shook Up" and many others here, Little Richard did "Kansas City" and "True Fine Mama," Larry Williams cut "Dizzy Miss Lizzy" and "Bad Boy," and lesser known rock icons The Collins Kids and Rose Maddox recorded here too. Today as Studio 56 it still does turnaway business: in 1993 Phil Spector produced a wall-of-sound session here featuring all his old players, but the tapes were never released.

THE RAINBOW
9001 Sunset Blvd.
West Hollywood

The restaurant next to the Roxy has drawn rock stars since its opening in 1973. It's so famous for its clientele—Led Zeppelin frequented it when it first opened, other hard rockers still do—that out-of-town rock fans often head straight for the Rainbow without even checking into their hotels. But it wasn't planned as a rockers' roost. When the Rainbow first opened, it was supposed to be a hangout for music biz heavies, drawing on the then music industry-heavy 9000 Sunset building across the street (See 9000 SUNSET) and other nearby music centers. And it worked for a little while—record company guys liked it, and came there, but then so did musicians looking to be signed. Pretty soon the execs fled, leaving just a bunch of guys with guitars and no contracts. But a mystique grew up around the place. Rockers supported it, the restaurant prospered, and today it's an acknowledged music biz landmark. (Other towns might find it odd to connect the word "landmark" with a building full of hard rockers. Not L.A.) This was formerly the Villanova, where Marilyn Monroe met Joe Dimaggio on a blind date.

RAJI'S
(former location)
6160 Hollywood Blvd.
Hollywood

This former Indian restaurant-turned-rock-club was run for years by the indomitable Dobbs, former manger of the Cathay De Grande (See CATHAY DE GRANDE), providing hard and traditional rock music in a comfortable setting (if you didn't mind the four-foot-thick support pillar in front of the stage). Many people played, some just hung out. Among the former: The Smithereens, Billy Bremner with Nick Lowe, Guns N' Roses, Treat Her Right, Screamin' Jay Hawkins, Panther Burns. Among the latter: The Replacements, The Cramps, Bruce Springsteen, Dwight Yoakam. The club is now razed, like the rest of the block.

RANCHO MUSIC
(former location)
2395 Westwood Blvd.
West Los Angeles

In 1965 there was a store here called Rancho Music that sold records and guitars. Former teenager Kathe Schreyer remembers coming here with her girlfriend looking for Beatles records, and the clerk, Bob Hite, laughing at them and telling them he was forming a blues band. "We laughed too," she said, "at the thought of Mr. Hite in a band. He was kind of big and wore velour zip-up turtlenecks." She also recalls that he had a jar on the counter where people were supposed to submit names for his band. Her entry, Big Bob and His Boys, didn't win, but Canned Heat did.

RCA RECORDS
(former location)
6363 Sunset Blvd.
Hollywood

When RCA Records was sold to Bertelsmann, the German corporate giant in 1988, they didn't change the record company's name, but they did change the logo on the building. This edifice housed the West Cost branch of that East Coast run company from the 1960s to 1994 when they moved to a swanky Beverly Hills address. More important historically is the recording studio downstairs. Now operated independently, it used to be RCA Studios, where The Rolling Stones recorded many of their songs, including "Satisfaction," "Heart of Stone," "19th Nervous Breakdown," "Paint It Black," and "Let's Spend the Night Together." The Jefferson Airplane recorded all of their sixties albums here except the first. And The Grateful Dead did *Anthem of the Sun* here. The Monkees recorded here too. No wonder RCA Records affixed "Recorded at the Music Center of the World" to their albums recorded here. Elvis Presley also recorded here in the 1970s. It must have been eerie to pass by in the wee hours of the morning and see fans keeping silent vigil at the door, standing for hours just waiting for the King to pass by.

RECORD STORES

Record stores were places where flat black discs encased in cardboard were sold from the 1920s to the 1980s. Today, though most only sell CDs and cassettes, they're still called record stores. Following are a few stores that still sell records. All sell CDs and cassettes too, but their stock of older material is what makes them noteworthy. They buy and sell recorded history.

Ear Candy, 6265 Sepulveda #11, Van Nuys
Founded in 1988 by record collector and musician Kip Brown (Shock, Little Girls), it stocks all formats for both record collectors and casual consumers. Closed Sundays.

Poo Bah, 1101 E. Walnut, Pasadena
When it opened in 1971 in the basement of the old Free Press Book Store in the then-crumbling Old Town district, Poo Bah became the magnet for record collectors and music lovers of this area. Its move to the house on Walnut sacrificed none of its charm (but a gigantic Beatle-memorabilia tower had to be disassembled), and today it still stands as a prime source of rare, and good, music.

Rhino Records, 1720 Westwood Blvd., Westwood
This all-format store—it includes both new and used merchandise—has well-stocked blues and oldies racks. Collectors' bins, parking lot sales, knowledgeable employees. Open seven days.

Rockaway, 2395 N. Glendale Blvd., Los Angeles
What began as a record collectors' store (they still have plenty of rarities) has evolved into a used-CD supermarket. Amazing turnover. Open seven days.

Another good vinyl source is www.hotplatters.com.

RECORD SWAP MEETS
Pasadena City College Flea Market
Colorado Blvd. and Hill Ave.
Pasadena

Record swap meets may actually have started in L.A.—especially because of our year-round temperate weather. The "Capitol" swap meet—so named for its stint in the Capitol Records parking lot in Hollywood from 1976 to 1978—began in the 1960s when the acronymically curious Society For The Preservation Of Early Recorded Music sold 78 rpm relics after their meetings at the International House of Pancakes on National and Sepulveda in West Los Angeles. In the early 1970s these buy-and-sell meets were invaded by younger collectors looking for rock and roll relics and their numbers swelled the meet to the point that it outgrew its grounds, leading to a nomadic existence that ended only in the mid-1980s when the collectors settled on the Pasadena City College grounds. The Pasadena meet, which is free, combines a regular flea market in the parking lot and record collectors in the subterranean driveway (in the shadows, so their wares won't melt). The meets are held the first Sunday of every month, 8:00 a.m. to 3:00 p.m. Two "record meets" have dominated the L.A. record (and now, CD) collectors market in the 1990s. Others crop up here and there, but the two main ones are:

Pasadena City College, Hill & Colorado, Pasadena
Not to be confused with the Pasadena Rose Bowl swap meet, which is held on the second Sunday of each month (and — fah! fah! — charges admission), this outdoor miracle of harmony and relaxedness has been meeting the FIRST Sunday of each month for more than ten years as a descendant of the Capitol Records record swap of the 1970s. (In the summer, come early: when records start melting, record-sellers go home.)

Buena Park Record Swap, 7530 Orangethorpe, Buena Park
The FOURTH Sunday of each month, this one meets indoors. Not as big as the Pasadena, but a good'un for other reasons: one, it's indoors, and two, it features recording artists available for autographs. Past visitors include Spencer Davis, Ella Mae Morse, Paul Peterson, and Jan & Dean.

RENDEZVOUS BALLROOM
(former location)
600 Ocean Front St.
Balboa

The concert hall that was here, home to the Stan Kenton band in the 1950s, burned down in 1965 just as it was taking on a new identity as the world center of surf music. Local (Fullerton) musician and surfer Dick Dale perfected, actually invented, with guitar manufacturer Leo Fender, a new sound, loud and wet with plenty of reverb, that made Dale THE act to see the summer of 1961, much of Dale's debut album *Surfer's Choice* was recorded here. His residency

here inspired countless other kids to form bands, and the surf music movement was born. After the 1962 fire, Dale moved to Harmony Park in Anaheim, taking up a residency that continued all through his national record-sales success (See HARMONY PARK). Bill Medley, pictured pointing to the site of the old club, said he and Bobby Hatfield got their start as The Righteous Brothers here; and no wonder, Medley's father was employed here as the hall's lighting engineer. A plaque in front of the Rendezvous apartments here commemorates the old hall.

RETAIL CLERKS HALL
8539 Stanton
Buena Park

It doesn't look like much now and hasn't hosted a rock & roll show in more than 30 years, but in 1963 this was the other locus of surf music excitement, the inland alternative to Balboa's Rendezvous Ballroom. (See RENDEZVOUS BALLROOM.) While in the summer of 1963 the Rendezvous had Dick Dale, the Retail Clerks had local monsters such as the Surfaris, the Sentinels, the Lively Ones, the Chantays, the Pyramids, the Ventures and the Beach Boys. The "house band," Eddie & The Showmen (not to be confused with the Norfolk, Virginia Showmen, who made "It Will Stand"), led by ex-Bel Airs guitarist Eddie Bertrand, made five sensational records for Liberty Records. (An 18-track CD was belatedly issued in 1997.)

RHINO RECORDS
1720 Westwood Blvd.
Westwood

Rhino was first a record store (See RECORD STORES) then a record label. The store was founded in the early 1970s by Richard Foos and Harold Bronson, young record collectors with no retail experience. Then located on Santa Monica Blvd. near Beverly Glen, the store grew steadily and branched off into a record label when Wild Man Fisher, a veteran of Frank Zappa's Bizarre Records, recorded "Go to Rhino Records," which Rhino issued as a single. More Rhino comedy releases followed and during the 1980s the label blossomed into America's premiere reissue label. It also developed new talent like Phranc, The Beat Farmers, House of Freaks, Billy Vera and the Beaters (whose "At This Moment" was Rhino's first number one record) and L.A. Rockabilly. In the 1990s, Rhino Records folded into the WEA organization, but it still issues outside projects. This location, its only L.A. store (there is a Rhino in Claremont which is not connected to this one), is a hep place with knowledgeable employees and a sporadic mid-week concert series that has included appearances by John Doe, Nick Lowe, Panther Burns, The Cowboy Junkies, Big Sandy & His Fly Rite Boys and The Sprague Brothers.

RANDY RHOADS GRAVE
Mountain View Cemetery
Highland & Waterman
San Bernadino

Randy Rhoads was a premier hard-rock guitarist who never reached his full potential, dying tragically at age twenty-five. Born December 6, 1956, to a musical family—his mother ran a music school—Rhoads took to the guitar at age seven, and ten years later joined Quiet Riot, a seminal L.A. hard rock band. Later in the 1970s he signed on to Ozzy Osbourne's band and played brilliantly on such albums as *Blizzard of Oz* and *Diary of a Madman.* Rhoads was a bright light on the rock scene when, on a break between concert dates in Orlando, Florida, on March 19, 1982, Osbourne's bus driver took Rhoads and wardrobe consultant Rachel Youngblood for a spin in a private plane. Aycock's playful "buzzing" of the band's bus caused the plane to clip a wing and crash to the ground, killing all aboard. Rhoads' nameplate in Mountain View is decorated with a guitar emblem and the Rolls-Royce "RR" emblem he adopted after his name. The crypt is placed up high near the ceiling to discourage enthusiastic fans from (however lovingly) taking souvenirs or writing inscriptions.

MINNIE RIPERTON GRAVE
Pierce Brothers Cemetery
1218 Glendon
Westwood

Chicago-born Minnie Riperton was famous for her five-octave singing range. She had operatic aspirations but found success in the pop world, first with the group Rotary Connection in

Chicago, then in 1975 with her own hit, "Lovin' You," produced by Stevie Wonder. She died of breast cancer on July 12, 1979 at the age of thirty-one. This cemetery has become a "tragic female death" center. Also here are Natalie Wood (drowned), actress Dominique Dunne (killed by her boyfriend), Playmate/actress Dorothy Stratten (killed by her husband), Heather O'Rourke (*Poltergeist* child who died on the operating table) and Marilyn Monroe. Stan Kenton and Buddy Rich are also here, as is Roy Orbison (See ROY ORBISON).

"ROCK AND ROLL" DENNY'S

7373 Sunset Blvd.
West Hollywood
Somehow, this Denny's restaurant, with the same bill of fare as every other Denny's in the nation, has become a magnet for rockers. It's just around the corner from the hard-rock Rock City News office, and draws musicians like Poison, The Jesus and Mary Chain, and deejay Rodney Bingenheimer (who can recall the night five girls from L.A. were eating here and decided to name their group The Go-Go's). On weekends after 2:00 a.m. (when clubs close) the clientele here is really something to see.

THE ROCK CORPORATION

(former location)
14310 Oxnard
Van Nuys
This rough-and-tumble club, poetically located across the street from a power-generating plant, provided a fairly unwholesome atmosphere in which local area rock bands could gain exposure during the 1970s. Among the players: Black Oak, The Knack, The Heaters, Van Halen, and The Rotters, whose underground hit, "Sit On My Face Stevie Nicks," died from lack of airplay.

JIMMIE RODGERS BEATING SITE

N. side of Renaldi Blvd.
W. of the 405 overpass,
Granada Hills
Jimmie Rodgers career started in 1957 with the bright folk-song hit "Honeycomb," progressed to TV, movie, and concert success, and ended here December 2, 1967. That night he exited the 405 freeway at Renaldi,

turned left, and stopped in response to headlight flashes from a car behind him. A man walked up, identified himself as an off-duty cop, accused Rodgers of cutting him off in traffic and savagely beat him into unconsciousness. No one really knows what happened—a drunk, rogue cop is the accepted story, though record industry people largely suspected it was related to Rodgers' departure from a reputedly gangster-based record company. Despite two hit records ("It's Over" and "Child Of Clay") that year, Rodgers did not return to the recording and concert trail after his recovery. He now writes, produces and occasionally performs in Branson, Missouri.

RODNEY BINGENHEIMER'S ENGLISH DISCO
(former location)
7561 Sunset Blvd.
Hollywood

Rodney Bingenheimer is a longtime L.A. scene figure, harking back to 1966 when he was Davy Jones' stand-in on "The Monkees." He hung around with Sonny and Cher (See MARTONI'S) and Sal Mineo dubbed him "Mayor of the Sunset Strip." The GTOs recorded "Rodney," a song about Bingenheimer, on their *Permanent Damage* album (1969). He opened this club in 1972 (his previous club, the E Club, was at 8171 Sunset, now La Toque restaurant) during the second British Invasion of the early 1970s (Bowie, Queen, Suzi Quatro, Sweet). It was the place to commingle with those rock stars and others: young Joan Jett was drawn here, along with visitors including Marc Bolan of T-Rex, Led Zeppelin, and a seriously out-of-place Elvis Presley, who was brought here by an RCA promotion man. Sometimes the club featured live music: in 1973, Sean Cassidy made his singing debut there as the opening act for Iggy Pop. Today, Bingenheimer is a deejay on KROQ-FM. He still recalls the time in 1972 when he and David Bowie cruised Hollywood High trying to meet girls. "The girls didn't like David," Rodney says. "Maybe it was because he was wearing a dress." The previous occupant of this site was Ooh Poo Pah Doo, a nightclub where bands' publicity photos were painted—wall-sized—on the front of the club for the week they played.

ROLLIN' ROCK RECORDS
(former location)
6918 Peach
Van Nuys

Rollin' Rock Records, the world-famous rockabilly label, was run from this garage/studio from the seventies to the mid-eighties. Founder Rockin' Ronny Weiser recorded rockabilly greats such as Ray Campi, Johnny Legend, Gene Vincent, Mac Curates, Tony Conn, Ronnie Mack, Jack Waukeen Cochran, Rip Masters, Jimmy Maslon and The Blasters (their Rollin' Rock album, *American Music* [1980], is a much-sought collector's item). He also led an impassioned band of "Rockabilly rebels" on "missions" throughout L.A., cheering people like Jerry Lee Lewis and Carl Perkins and denouncing disco and other forms of music he found non-rocking. Weiser's crazed Rollin' Rock magazine (1971-1978)

was a rabid journal of fanaticism and non sequiturs that crusaded for rock and roll with near-demented fervor. His immigrant's zeal (born in Italy, he became an American citizen in 1979) and multiple enthusiasms led him to offer free magazine subscriptions to rockabilly fans behind the Iron Curtain, and to plant a grove of trees in Israel for Gene Vincent. Rollin' Rock Records' output didn't sell substantially in America, but it was very influential among a lot of just-developing musicians, including The Cramps and The Stray Cats. The label had its greatest success in Europe, where most of its acts toured. Ironically, Weiser slowed down his rockabilly output in the early 1980s, just as The Stray Cats-led rockabilly revival exploded. He now lives in Las Vegas. In 1997, High Tone Records began issuing his catalog, starting with The Blasters album and a compilation of Jimmie Lee Maslon tracks. (Maslon now owns the Ahi-Nama label in North Hollywood, specializing in Cuban music.)

LINDA RONSTADT'S FRONT PORCH (1970)
122 W. Hart St.
Venice
(Do Not Disturb Occupants)

Difficult to spot because it now sports two front doors not one, in 1970 Linda Ronstadt, who was living here, gathered a bunch of her friends to be photographed by Henry Diltz for the back cover of the *Linda Ronstadt & The Stone Poneys Vol. 3* album. Easily spottable are her neighbors Tim Buckley (right), LA scenemaker Rodney Bingenheimer (toppish), photographer Ed Careff (hunched, top left) and Capitol labelmates Hedge & Donna (lower right).

THE ROXY
9009 Sunset Blvd.
West Hollywood
The Roxy has a heavy record business lineage. Opened as a nightclub in 1973 by current owners Elmer Valentine (who also runs the Whisky) and Lou Adler (the Mamas and the Papas' record producer, who founded Ode Records and ran the Monterey Pop Festival) along with club owner

Chuck Landis and Elliot Roberts of Geffen-Roberts management, the Roxy was designed to loosen the Troubadour's stranglehold on better, i.e. non hard-rock acts, and succeeded. Opened amid great fanfare with Neil Young, the club prospered for several years until in 1978 record sales took a downturn and clubs found it tough sledding. A succession of identities followed and the club settled in the mid-1980s on the current format of renting out to independent promoters. Acts that played here? Davie Bowie, Bruce Springsteen, Bob Marley, Frank Zappa, Pee Wee Herman, Prince—it's a superstar venue that holds four hundred people. (The upstairs private club, On the Rox, has remained an exclusive music biz hangout through all the downstairs changes.)

ROXBURY DRIVE
(former location)
Sunset & Roxbury
Sunset Strip

Foremost on Roxbury Drive is the Roxbury Club, established in 1990 and closed in mid 1997, that featured solid middle-drawing acts. The building originally housed Preston Sturges's Players club (1940-1953), and was the Imperial Gardens restaurant, and The Boss Club, one of the first Springsteen-only discos, and deejay Rodney Bingenhemer's 1966 Club, in 1986. Not so visible on Roxbury, up the road at 8233, is the former home of record entrepreneur Tom Ayers. In the 1960s he produced "Hot Pastrami" by The Dartells and The Five Americans' "Western Union." Bingenheimer remembers bringing newcomer David Bowie up to Ayers' house in 1970 to meet the singer Ayers was managing, Gene Vincent. A tape of a Bowie/Vincent jam session recorded in Ayers' living room is played annually on Bingenheimer's KROQ radio show.

SANTA MONICA CIVIC AUDITORIUM
Pico Blvd. & Main St.
Santa Monica

In constant use since its construction in 1958, it has hosted countless rock shows and has seen a few rock music movies. In 1964, *The T.A.M.I Show* (Teenage Awards Music International), featuring The Rolling Stones, The Beach Boys, Jan and Dean, James Brown, and Marvin Gaye, was shot

here. And in 1979, equally memorably but for different reasons—the acts were spit upon and the cameras were in cages—it was the site of *Urgh! A Music War*, featuring The Go-Go's, The Cramps, Stiv Bators and several other new wavers. Springsteen played here, CSNY, Prince, Bob Dylan—basically everybody who was hot and on the way to the top.

SCRIVNER'S DRIVE-IN RESTAURANT
(former location)
Sunset & Cahuenga
Hollywood

In 1956, KPOP dejay Art Laboe began an after-school broadcast from this site and it swelled to become L.A.'s highest-rated radio show ever. Every contemporary star on the planet stopped by: Sam Cooke, Ricky Nelson, Little Richard, Chuck Berry, Jackie Wilson, The Crickets and The Teddy Bears. Elvis Presley even came by once, but declined to go on the air. Inspired by the number of requests he got from high schoolers who were sentimental for old records, Laboe originated the concept of "oldies but goodies" record reissues here (See ORIGINAL SOUND RECORDS). Scrivner's was torn down for a gas station in the sixties and then rebuilt in 1988 as a Jack-in-the-Box fast food restaurant. (Art Laboe's star on the Walk of Fame is on the southwest corner of Sunset and Highland).

SECURITY FIRST NATIONAL BANK
(former location)
6302 Van Nuys
Van Nuys

In 1966 Harry Nilsson worked the clerical night shift at this building, or one just like it at this address. In the day he was writing songs for the Monkees ("Cuddly Toy"), Ronettes ("Paradise"), and himself. By 1967 fame beckoned and bank work became a thing of the past. Nilsson is buried at Pierce Bros. Valley Oak Memorial Park in Westlake Village.

SEVEN EIGHTY THREE BEL-AIR ROAD
Bel-Air

This house, built by film thrush Jeanette McDonald, had two more shots of music fame — as John and Michelle Phillips' residence in the 1960s (much discussed in his book Papa John,) and later when it was rented by Sly Stone (moved in 1970: evicted 1973.) Stone recorded much of the *There's A Riot Going On* album in the attic studio (installed by Phillips) here.

SEVENTH & MAIN

Downtown Los Angeles

Atop this row of stores on Skid Row on March 12, 1987, U2 did an unauthorized rooftop concert that became their video for "Where The Streets Have No Name." Like they expected, the cops shut them down, but their daring-do was actually more curious than meaningful—theirs was simply a self-conscious restaging of the London rooftop scene in The Beatles film *Let It Be*.

SHAKEY'S PIZZA

(former location)
Gayley & Weyburn
Westwood

In 1971, brothers Ron & Russel Mael made their first paid performance here, when it was a Shakey's Pizza (they were paid with pizzas). The act, first called Halfnelson, then Sparks, quickly went on to world fame.

SHANGRILA RECORDING STUDIO

(former location)
30065 Morning View Dr.
Zuma Beach

The Band holed up here in the early 1970s when the right half of the main house was a recording studio. Here they recorded *Northern Lights–Southern Cross*, mixed *The Basement Tapes*, did parts for *The Last Waltz*, and outside projects by Neil Diamond (*Beautiful Noise*)

and Hirth Martinez (*Hirth From Earth*). The smaller cottage to the left was said to be a home for tv's "Mr. Ed," though this may have just been a "pipe dream."

DEL SHANNON DEATH SITE
15519 Saddleback
Canyon Country
(Do Not Disturb Occupants)

Del Shannon first rose to national prominence in 1961 with his self-penned song "Runaway." He had several subsequent hits in the mid-1960s, but he never quite emerged from the shadow of that first one. Though he was still doing concerts, collecting royalties, and planning to record with Jeff Lynne and Tom Petty, Shannon, a recovering alcoholic, called it quits the night of February 8, 1990, committing suicide in this newly-bought home outside of Santa Clarita, forty miles north of L.A. He was cremated and his ashes scattered.

SHARON SHEELEY
FORMER RESIDENCE
Four Gables Apartments
Fountain & Harper
West Hollywood

Teenaged Sharon Sheeley lived with her mother in this castle-like corner apartment when she was the center of the L.A. rock and roll scene in 1959. She wrote "Poor Little Fool" for Ricky Nelson, "Something Else" for Eddie Cochran, and "Hurry Up" for Ritchie Valens and she was Cochran's girlfriend (See EDDIE COCHRAN). Her apartment was the gathering spot for rock royalty: Cochran, Buddy Holly and The Crickets, Gene Vincent, Ricky Nelson, Dion and The Everly Brothers were among the rockers big and small who made Sheeley's place the center of their social world in L.A. But then her life took a tragic turn. On April 17, 1960, Sharon was traveling in England with Cochran and Vincent when their cab crashed, crushing Vincent's leg, breaking Sharon's neck and killing Eddie. She lay in a hospital bed for six months, recovering slowly after doctors gave her a ten percent chance of pulling through. When she was well enough, she resumed songwriting and with Jackie DeShannon wrote "Dum Dum" and "Heart in Hand" for Brenda Lee, and "The Great Impostor" for The Fleetwoods. In 1962 she married deejay (and future "Shindig" host) Jimmy O'Neill and met a new generation of rockers, including The Beatles, Peter and Gordon, Jeff Beck and Jimi Hendrix. Today she lives in Sherman Oaks with her son. Her life story would make a great book.

SHELLEY'S MANNE-HOLE
(former location)
1608 Cahuenga
Hollywood

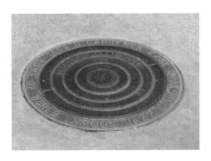

From 1960 through 1974, this was the site of Los Angeles' most eminent jazz club. Nationally known jazz players headlined, often backed by Hollywood's greatest studio musicians — musicians who excelled in rock and jazz alike. Studio aces like Larry Bunker (Spector, Fifth Dimension), Tommy Tedesco

(Spector, Beach Boys, and just about everybody else) and Carol Kaye (Spector, Motown, Beach Boys) all turned up on this bandstand at least once. Headliners included Bill Evans, Miles Davis, John Coltrane, and virtually every other major figure in modern jazz. The club was run by Shelly Manne, who, although born in New York, was the epitome of West Coast cool jazz drumming from the early fifties until his death in 1984. More relevant to this book, Manne also recorded with rockers such as Frank Zappa (*Lumpy Gravy*), and Tom Waits (*Small Change, Foreign Affairs*, and *One From The Heart*). In a way, the club was succesfull in its bid for immortality: embedded in the sidewalk outside the current cash-exchange at this location is a "man-hole" comemmorating the world-renowned club.

SHERMAN OAKS GALLERIA
Ventura & Sepulveda
Sherman Oaks

When Frank and Moon Zappa wrote "Valley Girl" about teenagers who hung out at malls, this was the place from which Moon drew her inspiration. This was also the mall where *Fast Times at Ridgemont High* was filmed.

SHERMAN SQUARE
ENTERTAINMENT CENTER
18430 Sherman Way
Reseda

During the roller-disco craze, a week didn't pass without hearing about Cher's celebrity-filled rollerskating parties at this place, located right across the street from the Country Club concert venue.

THE SHRINE AUDITORIUM
665 West Jefferson
Los Angeles

Constructed in 1927, this Moorish-style auditorium has been host to many major rock and roll shows, not to mention to King Kong, who was chained up on the Shrine's stage in the original movie. During the 1950s, promoter Gene Norman held black "Jubilees" here, with acts like Big Jay

McNeely and Wynonie Harris. And Elvis Presley played here on June 8, 1956. During the 1960s, Frank Zappa held a series of multi-media, colorfully chaotic "Freak Outs" here, nominally at the Shrine, but actually at the nearby Exposition Hall. The one on August 13, 1966 featured The County Five, The West Coast Pop Art Experimental Band, seven-year-old soul singer Little Gary Ferguson, The Factory (an early Lowell George band) and Kenny Dino, whose "Your Ma Said You Cried In Your Sleep Last Night" was recut in 1990 by Robert Plant. Other promoters used that spacious hall to great advantage too: some shows, like one in 1969 featuring the Moody Blues, Ten Years After and Jeff Beck, were set up on three stages so the music was nonstop. The Grateful Dead played two famous (among Deadheads) shows here November 10 & 11, 1967. Jimi Hendrix's February 10, 1968 appearance is now the stuff of legend. Jefferson Airplane, The Yardbirds, The Velvet Underground, The Who, The Doors, Quicksilver, Steve Miller, James Brown, Joe Cocker—the list of rock bands that appeared here goes on forever. The Shrine is also used for the Grammy Awards, MTV Awards, American Music Awards and other shows.

SLASH RECORDS
7381 Beverly Blvd.
West Hollywood

Built up from a popular punk/art magazine of the late 1970s, Slash was the mainstay L.A. rock label of that era, signing The Germs, The Blasters, X, The Gun Club, and The Flesheaters. Later additions Los Lobos, Green on Red, The Bodeans, and The Violent Femmes served to further validate the label's artist vision. (Don't show up here. Send a tape.)

SLAUSON AVENUE
Los Angeles

This is a main drag through South L.A., equivalent to Whittier Boulevard in East L.A. The street was the subject of local dance hit, "Do the Slauson," by Round Robin in 1963.

P.F. SLOAN FORMER RESIDENCE
6290 Del Valle Dr.
Los Angeles
(Do Not DIsturb Occupants)

New York-born Phillip "P.F." Sloan wrote "Eve Of Destruction" in this, his family's house, in which he spent his youth and teens. Sloan is known for writing many hit songs (often with partner Steve Barri) for other artists — "You Baby," "Secret Agent Man," and "Where Were You (When I Needed You)" — while his own excellent versions remained unappreciated until many years later. (Tunesmith Jimmy Webb wrote a song about him, "P.F. Sloan," in the late 1960s.) He also strummed the opening for the Mamas & Papas' "California Dreamin'." Reclusive for much of the 1970s and 1980s, Sloan re-emerged in the mid-1990s with a new album and personal appearances.

SMOKEY JOE'S CAFE
(former location)
Beverly & La Cienega
West Hollywood

SMOKEY JOE'S BARBEQUE
12851 Riverside Dr.
North Hollywood

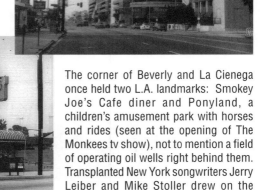

The corner of Beverly and La Cienega once held two L.A. landmarks: Smokey Joe's Cafe diner and Ponyland, a children's amusement park with horses and rides (seen at the opening of The Monkees tv show), not to mention a field of operating oil wells right behind them. Transplanted New York songwriters Jerry Leiber and Mike Stoller drew on the former when they wrote "Smokey Joe's Cafe" for The Robins in 1956. "Smokey Joe's Cafe" became a hit, The Robins became The Coasters and in 1980, Smokey Joe's and Ponyland became the Beverly Center shopping mall. Smokey Joe's Barbecue in North Hollywood is a still-standing branch of the original restaurant.

SONY MUSIC
24th & Colorado
Santa Monica
Sony, Columbia, and Epic Records are accessible on the corner of the huge Sony complex and park. (Don't show up with your guitar, send a demo).

SOUND CITY
15456 Cabrito
Van Nuys
When Vox Amps opened this studio as Vox Recorders in 1964, it was in the boondocks. It still is, and claims a mighty impressive 'track' record of clientele: Rage Against The Machine and Tool; Nirvana recorded *nevermind* here; Tom Petty's been using it for, oh, 20 years; Fleetwood Mac cut their

big comeback album (and part of *Rumours*) here; and this is where The Grateful Dead cut *Terraplane Station*. Counterbalancing the good vibes, Charles Manson cut his demos here. It's been owned since 1969 by Tom Skeeter who proudly notes that the decor hasn't changed since 1972.

SPACELAND
1717 Silverlake Blvd.
Silverlake
Truly a new-scene landmark, this club has been the launching pad for the widely-discussed and mostly unhatched "Silverlake Sound" (or was it the Los Feliz Beat?). The Dust Bros. production team scouted and signed and showcased new bands here for their Bong Load Record company. Beck hit, and soon the Dust brothers were as hot as that Was brother was. All sorts of national bands play here, like Los Straitjackets and Flat Duo Jets. Also non-earthbound ones like Man Or Astroman?

SPARK RECORDS
(former location)
8567 Melrose Ave.
West Hollywood

Spark Records moved to this building in June 1955, from its original location at 1119 Crenshaw. The label, co-owned by the songwriting team of Leiber & Stoller and record industry figure Lester Sill (Duane Eddy, Philles Records, Screen Gems Music), made its biggest mark with "Riot In Cell Block #9" by the Robins. (See SMOKEY JOE'S CAFE.)

SPIRIT ALBUM COVER SITE
Sunset Highland Motel
6830 Sunset Blvd.
Hollywood

Spirit was an L.A. band whose songs "I've Got a Line on You" and "Fresh Garbage" became FM-radio staples in the early 1970s, making them one of the first star bands of the decade. They posed themselves on a staircase leading down from the top floor of this then(!) seedy hotel right across the street from Hollywood High School for the cover of their second album, *The Family That Plays Together.*

THE STARWOOD
(former location)
Santa Monica Blvd. & Crescent Heights
West Hollywood

Two great nightclubs occupied this site. The first was PJ's, a rather square supper club that went on the map with house bandleader Trini Lopez's nationwide hit album *Trini Lopez—Live at PJ's.* (The Standells recorded live at PJ's as did the Bobby Fuller Four and the Sin SayShuns.)   During the 1970s, this was The Starwood, the hardrock palace for Slade, Bachman-Turner Overdrive, Van Halen, Black Oak Arkansas, Quiet Riot, Cheap Trick, and hundreds of other dissimilar bands including Devo, The Knack, The Blasters, bluesman Roy Brown, Johnny Cougar, Fear, The Go-Go's, Black Flag, Peter Tosh—you never knew who'd appear there next. Memories abound. There was Paul Kossoff's last gig here with Backstreet Crawler, the night before he died. Or the time Rick Derringer got a police escort to The Starwood after playing the Santa Monica Civic. And the nights in the early eighties when you'd see members of Mötley Crüe walking around looking way out of place in their dated glam-rock gear. And what about Zolar X? They played sporadically but got into clubs free just for having shaved heads, silver skin and space suits. But, like all rock clubs it seems, The Starwood had to close. Neighbors' complaints about rudeness and lewdness ultimately did the trick (as did Starwood owner Eddie Nash's ongoing battles with the law). The place shut decisively in 1982 and was partially dismantled and changed into a mall.

STEPHEN STILLS RANCH (1968)

1174 Old Topanga Canyon Road
Topanga

In 1968 Stephen Stills, still in Buffalo Springfield, rented a ranch off this road. On the night of March 28th, police were summoned by neighbors annoyed by noise, raided the house and arrested 13 partygoers for marijuana posession, including Eric Clapton, Neil Young, Jim Messina and Richie Furay. (The Santa Monica Evening Outlook reported the other arrestees as Nancy Furay, Susan Haffey, Karen Harvey, Mary Hughes, Eugene Sarns, Linda Sontag, Linda Stevens, Hannah R. Stills, and Talitha Stills.) Party host Stills escaped through a back window and arranged for legal and financial aid. (The Outlook reported that the defendants rode to Malibu Court "in chauffer-driven limousines and accompanied by high-priced attorneys.") Charges were eventually reduced to disturbing the peace, and nobody went to jail. The ranch was later rented by many So. Cal music dignitaries, including Eagle Bernie Leadon and Neil Young producer David Briggs.

STONE CANYON

a road in Bel Air

Rick Nelson formed his Stone Canyon Band in the early 1970s, when it seemed like every L.A. band was sporting droopy mustaches and singing about the West. Did Nelson choose the Stone Canyon name because it sounded appropriately rustic? If so, it was his little joke, since there are no tumbleweeds or cowpokes on this slice of expensive Los Angeles real estate.

STUDIO Z
(former location)
8040 Archibald
Cucamonga

Not really the same building—the original edifice was torn down—but at least the same address as Frank Zappa's Studio Z, the recording studio where he worked, and got arrested, in 1964. Zappa bought this recording studio and turned it into custom recording business. When business was slow he worked on his own music and the score for the little-seen Timothy Carey film *The World's Greatest Sinner.* The enterprise generated so little money that when a plain-clothes policeman came in and asked Zappa to make a "blue" recording, Zappa gleefully complied. The resultant grunt-and-gasp record was then picked up by the detective and the cuffs were slapped on Frank. He fought the prosecution, paid a fine and left Cucamonga for good.

SUNSET GRILL
7439 Sunset Blvd.
Hollywood

Subject of the Don Henley song "Sunset Grill." Now closed.

SUNSET MARQUIS HOTEL
1200 Alta Loma
West Hollywood

This hotel has catered to musicians with music-biz savvy and discretion for at least two decades. Depeche Mode's Gahan endured both a suicide attempt and an arrest here. The pool area can be a great spot for star-watching—if you're registered.

SUNSET STRIP BILLBOARDS
Sunset Strip

In 1967 Elektra Records president Jac Holzman took out a billboard on Sunset for the first Doors album—and from then on the race was on. Immediately every record company—their artists, actually—were fighting for space there and recording contracts came with automatic billboard provisions—the only negotiable point was how long the ad would run. It was exciting to watch that tableau unfold in the 1970s. As soon as the Leon Russell one went down, the Steve Miller one came up. And what about The Beatles' billboard for Abbey Road? Their heads poked above the top of the board and someone cut off Paul's—did that

mean he was really dead? And poor Ringo Starr, his 1974 billboard for Ringo had tons of lights on it, but it came right during the energy crunch and he got lambasted for it. Then there was the one with Swamp Dogg's interesting challenge, "If you don't like my album, pucker up while I'm backing up." The "crash" of the late seventies, when record sales fell precipitously, quashed record companies fascination with billboards and when business picked up, the rock billboards didn't reappear (though in the 1990s a few trickled back).

SUNSET TOWERS
(former location)
8358 Sunset Blvd.
West Hollywood

Out to outclass his brother (See PHIL'S DINER), at least in choice of album-cover buildings, Don Everly issued his *Sunset Towers* (1976) album with this beautiful 1930s Art Deco building on the cover. The

record sold poorly, the building's been remodeled (now its The Argyle) and Don's back singing with his brother Phil in the Everly Brothers. (His daughter briefly married Axl Rose of Guns N' Roses in 1990.)

TAIL O' THE PUP
329 N. San Vicente
West Hollywood

After thirty years on La Cienega, this revered hot dog stand was relocated to the boondocks of San Vicente to make way for the urgently needed Ma Maison Hotel. Though it is primarily known as a shutterbug stop for tourists, it also shows up in rock videos and on album covers.

THEE EXPERIENCE
(former location)
Sunset Blvd. & Sierra Bonita
Hollywood

Thee Experience was a popular club of the late 1960s on whose front wall was painted a huge Jimi Hendrix head—you walked in through Hendrix's mouth. Hendrix used to jam here as did members of Led Zeppelin, Quicksilver and Len Fagen (who used to book the Coconut Teaszer). The Blues Magoos, The Bonzo Dog Band, Alice Cooper and many other bands played here on their way up. In 1969, Pamela Des Barres (then Miss Pamela of the GTOs) attended a Bo Diddley show here and met

Led Zeppelin's Jimmy Page, leading to the lengthy romance described in her book, *I'm With The Band*. Some of the band's salty escapades at Thee Experience are described in the book *Hammer of the Gods* by Stephen Davis.

WILLIE MAE "BIG MAMA" THORNTON GRAVE

Inglewood Park Cemetery
720 E. Florence
Inglewood

A big woman with a growling voice, Big Mama Thornton made her mark in 1953 with "Hound Dog," a song written for her by L.A. area songwriters Jerry Leiber and Mike Stoller. (In 1956 the song got to Elvis Presley, though not through Big Mama's version— he heard it in Las Vegas performed by Freddie Bell and The Bellboys.) She continued to enjoy popularity as a blues singer through the sixties, seventies and eighties playing L.A. blues clubs (The Ash Grove, The Troubadour and others) and festivals around the world. Just before her death Thornton appeared at Club Lingerie in Hollywood. Suffering from cancer, she wasn't "big" anymore—she had shrunk to near skeletal size—but she still belted the blues. Thornton is buried with two other people in this roadside grave. Exactly what the arrangement means is not clear, but it's pretty certain it doesn't mean she died with an excess of money.

TOPANGA CANYON

East of Malibu

Topanga is a little pocket of 1970 tucked back away in the mountains of L.A. The hippie ethic and nineties style, makes for a lifestyle where patchouli oil and fax machines actually do mix. Its musical history goes way back. Woody Guthrie maintained a home here in the 1940s, so did Lord Buckley. TV's "Waltons" star Will Geer

lived out his days running annual music festivals here through the early 1980s. And some locals claim Joni Mitchell as a lady of their canyon even through she never lived here. The most famous local landmark was the Topanga Corral, at 2034 Topanga Canyon Rd. Now leveled, it was a major Los Angeles venue in the 1970s, and is remembered for shows by Canned Heat, bluesmen Pee Wee Crayton and Big Joe Turner, Spirit, Spanky and Our Gang and the for the legendary night Neil Young, Joni Mitchell and The Eagles played together. Right behind the Corral was a cabin that Jim Morrison bought for his wife Pamela—the roadhouse of The Doors' "Roadhouse Blues." The leader of Canned Heat, Bob "The Bear" Hite lived at 701 Topanga Canyon Road during the 1970s. A massive man with a record collection to match, Hite's dabbling with drugs was his undoing, he died of an overdose after a gig at The Palomino. (Years earlier, Canned Heat's guitarist Al "Owl" Wilson had died of an overdose in Hite's yard here.) The old house was destroyed in a flood. Then there was the Spirit house on Cuesta Cala Road.

Jay Ferguson, Mark Andes, and John Locke of that formative L.A. Band lived there, along with rock Doc Barry Hansen (See PICO AND SEPULVEDA) in the late sixties. (Spirit's "Topanga Windows" was written here.) And there was also the rickety hillside house that Vince Furnier lived in while he was becoming Alice Cooper. Early in 1968 there was a famous "bust" at the Stephen Stills Ranch (See STEPHEN STILLS RANCH) ranch, which netted Eric Clapton, Jim Messina and Neil Young. (Two years later Young read a film treatment called *After the Gold Rush,* written by Topanga resident Dean Stockwell, and wrote a soundtrack for it. The movie was never made, but the soundtrack made a great Neil Young album.) And speaking of hillside domiciles, The Byrds' *Notorious Byrd Brothers* album cover was shot at a stop on a Topanga horse trail. The horse in the fourth stall was not put there to mock the recently-departed David Crosby (who had just left The Byrds to join Crosby, Stills and Nash). It just walked in.

TOPS RECORDS
(former location)
5810 South Normandie
Los Angeles

Breathes there a record collector so perverse that he or she collects Tops Records? Even in that maniacal discipline, it's doubtful. Tops manufactured "soundalike" imitations of popular records of the late fifties—twelve songs on an album for only a dollar—and were they awful! The names of the artists were not listed on the albums—probably for their safety—and listening to these abominations many years after their departure can still bring a tear to a music-lover's eye. (An exception is George Jones' hot rendering of "Heartbreak Hotel" and "Blue Suede Shoes," done as Hank Smith.) This was also the address for Modern Records, which issued Tops (See MODERN).

TOWER RECORDS
8801 Sunset Blvd.
West Hollywood

Formerly Earl "Madman" Muntz's car stereo outlet, this large warehouse became the home of the world's largest record store when Tower Records opened in 1971. They pioneered the wall-sized reproduction of album covers, they held frequent promotions in the store and in their parking lot, and the place mushroomed into a nationwide chain.

TRAVEL TOWN TRANSPORTATION MUSEUM
Griffith Park
4730 Crystal Springs Drive
Burbank

Several album covers were shot in here, including *Jan and Dean's Greatest Hits Volume 3* and Mama Cass's *The Road Is No Place for a Lady.* Also, The Beach boys posed on a train here for the cover of the sheet music for "Sloop John B." At least one "Monkees" episode was shot here as well.

THE TRIP
(former location)
8572 Sunset Blvd.
West Hollywood

One of the seminal clubs of the Sunset Strip in the mid-sixties, The Trip featured good bands, including The Velvet Underground, The Paul Butterfield Blues Band, The Byrds, The Turtles, and frequently appearances by The Modern Folk Quartet. (On their initial road trip, the Velvet Underground got their only encouraging West Coast reaction from The Trip audience, undeterred by headliner Frank Zappa's unkind onstage assessments of them. Years later, in the height of irony, Lou Reed presided over Zappa's posthumous induction into the Rock & Roll Hall Of Fame.) Donovan played a week here in 1966 when his music was changing from folk to psychedelic (hence "The Trip," on the *Sunshine Superman* album). Upstairs above The Trip was the Interlude, where Lenny Bruce sometimes performed. The building, long torn down, originally housed Gene Norman's Crescendo, a very popular jazz club of the 1950s. The site is now a vacant lot.

TROPICANA MOTEL
(former location)
8585 Santa Monica Blvd.
West Hollywood

Torn down amid much sadness in 1988, this motel served as the rock and roll oasis of the sixties, seventies and eighties. Once owned by baseballer Sandy Koufax, the place was run-down but elegant—and cheap—when Jim Morrison lived there, and when Tom Waits rented a bungalow in the back behind it, and his pal Chuck E. ("Chuck E's in Love") Weiss rented a small room beneath an adjoining stairwell. The Clash, The Sex Pistols, The Jam, The Damned, The Byrds, Jackie Wilson, Iggy Pop, Blondie, The Ramones, and Bruce Springsteen all stayed here—the Trop was your first stop on your way up the rock and roll ladder, as well as a place to stay once you made it.

THE TROUBADOUR
9081 Santa Monica Blvd.
West Hollywood

The Troubadour's stage held the great names of the sixties and seventies rock—Springsteen, Jackson Browne, Elton John—during its reign as the "smart" rock showplace of L.A., but ultimately the changing nature of nightclub contracts did it in. The Troub started as a coffeehouse on La Cienega in the late 1950s, and moved to this location in 1961. It grew with the folk music boom: The New Christy Minstrels, Phil Ochs, Odetta and the like graced its stage. By the late

1960's "adult" rock grew in importance and the Troub corralled it all. By 1970, when Elton John made his world-shaking debut here—the whole world, it seemed, beheld his triumphant arrival—the Troub had a stranglehold on the music scene. You had to play here, and many did: Van Morrison, Carole King, Paul Butterfield, Neil Diamond, Arlo Guthrie, Janis Joplin, Judy Collins, Miles Davis, Bo Diddley—the list is nearly endless. They played two shows a night, six nights a week which was great for customers, who could come back and bring friends to see someone they enjoyed, but that booking policy ultimately led to the club's downfall. The music business was changing. When the Roxy opened in 1973 offering musicians a chance to play one and two-night stints in a prestigious setting, they trampled each other to get there, leaving the Troub to rot. And rot it did. During the late seventies it looked like the Troubadour would fold, but then owner Doug Weston took a drastic musical gamble and won. Heavy metal was getting big and Weston went with it, turning the old acoustic folk music den into one of the city's premiere hard rock venues. In the 1990s the club returned to a versatile booking policy. Any number of incidents occurred here—Weston should write a book—but probably the most famous was the night in 1974 when John Lennon was ejected for rowdiness after he entered with a Kotex taped to his forehead—just weeks after he and Elton John had joined Dr. John onstage for an impromptu jam.

TROUPERS HALL
1543 North La Brea
Hollywood

Once a grand old hall for thespians, this place also has a rock and roll history. Does anyone remember The Grateful Dead playing here in 1966? Well, then, what about the Radio Free Hollywood show in 1975? Local bands The Motels, The Dogs, and The Pop rented the place to prove that the local scene was alive and valid, and drew turnaway crowds. It's also fondly remembered as the site of Pumping Piano Productions' 1980-1985 New Year's parties, which featured, among others, Joe King Carrasco, The Blasters, Screamin' Jay Hawkins, Bull Moose Jackson, Cannibal and the Headhunters, The Beat Farmers, Jo-El Sonnier and many more.

TTG STUDIO
(former location)
1441 N. McCadden Place
Hollywood

Built in 1927 as a Knights of Columbus hall, this was used as a recording facility in various hands (Conway, ABC, Radio Recorders). In its heyday in the late 1960s (under then-owner Ami Hadani) as TTG, the first Mothers Of Invention album was cut here, as was the Ventures' "Wild Thing" album, and the single version of the Beach Boys' "Help Me Rhonda." It now houses a photo-research firm.

BIG JOE TURNER GRAVE
Roosevelt Memorial Park
Gardena

Big Joe Turner indisputably earned his sobriquet "The Boss of the Blues." He learned about music in his hometown of Kansas City, and then brought his belting blues to New York, setting that town on its ear with a history-making performance at Carnegie Hall in 1938. Moving to Los Angeles, he appeared in Duke Ellington's all-black musical Jump For Joy at the Mayan Theater in 1941 and continued to make records and tour the world the rest of his life. During the 1950's Turner was one of the few old blues-men to bridge the gap between jazz and rock and roll. His "Shake, Rattle and Roll" set the standard for others to match (Bill Haley's version was a fine cover) and he followed it with "Honey Hush," "Flip, Flop and Fly," and many more. He played everywhere in L.A. during the sixties and seventies: The Ash Grove, The Parisian Room, The Palladium, The Golden Bear, The Starwood, The Fox-Venice, The Topanga Corral and made a highly memorable appearance at Club Lingerie in 1982, backed by members of The Blasters and The Lee Allen Orchestra. When Big Joe died November 24, 1985, it came as no shock, what was surprising was how long he had survived, carrying as he did four hundred pounds on his frame. Contemporary Bull Moose Jackson explained Joe's longevity by saying: "Remember how they built Packards back in the thirties? You could run one into a wall and then drive off. That's how they built Big Joe."

IKE & TINA TURNER FORMER RESIDENCE
4263 Olympiad Drive, View Park
Baldwin Hills

Ike & Tina Turner lived at this hilltop residence from their heyday in the 1970s until they divorced. Ike was a pioneer in rock & roll history — as a guitarist, songwriter, arranger, and talent-seeker (he discovered and produced many artists for Sun and Chess Records in the 1950s, and it was his band that made "Rocket 88," often cited as the first rock & roll record, credited to Ike's singer Jackie Brenston) he stands among the giants. Today Tina is an international star and lives in Europe with a new mate, and Ike and his wife Jeanette tour the U.S. and Europe with the new Ike Turner Revue. (This house was used in the film *What's Love Got To Do With It*.)

UNITED ARTISTS RECORDS
(former location)
6920 Sunset Blvd.
Hollywood

Liberty Records moved here in 1961, enjoyed many, many hits (after absorbing Imperial Records in 1964 its roster included Johnny Rivers, Jan & Dean, Jackie DeShannon, The Hollies, Gary Lewis & The Playboys, Cher, the Spencer Davis Group, Gordon Lightfoot, Jay & The Americans, the Ventures, Sandy Nelson and more!) and was bought out before the decade's end by United Artists Records. UA had a great assortment of hit acts through the 1970s — Kenny Rogers, ELO, Crystal Gayle, War, Don McLean, then was swallowed by EMI in the 1980s. (Trivia note: late 70s UA labels orange sunset design symbolized their location here at Orange & Sunset.)

UNITED/WESTERN RECORDING STUDIOS
United 6050 Sunset Blvd., Hollywood
Western 6000 Sunset Blvd., Hollywood

These two adjacent studios are now operated under the Oceanway banner. Sinatra, Ellington, Basie, all the biggies used them, but rock recording is our area, so among their clients were Sam Cooke, Sonny & Cher, Jan & Dean, Mamas & Papas, Simon & Garfunkel, The Association, Michael Jackson, Rolling Stones, Toto, Bonnie Raitt, Kim Carnes and The Blasters. Brian Wilson cut most of the Beach Boys stuff here, including *Pet Sounds*. If anyone asks where the LA Rock and Roll Hall of Fame is, send 'em here.

UNION STATION
800 North Alameda
Los Angeles

Site of many videos and album covers (Bonnie Raitt's *Taking My Time* is one) this is also the station Elvis pulls into with much fanfare in the video release *Elvis '56*.

RITCHIE VALENS GRAVE
San Fernando Mission Cemetery
San Fernando

Ritchie Valens' career was a comet across the sky of Los Angeles. That a local teenager could leap into the same league as Elvis in 1958 was something most L.A. kids never imagined—but for a Hispanic kid to make it, with a song sung in Spanish ("La Bamba"), well, the impact on the Mexican-American community was immeasurable. Its grief was especially great then when that same young hero died suddenly in a plane crash after less than a year of stardom. A whole generation of Latinos grew up feeling the void left by Ritchie's death.

Ritchie grew up in Pacoima and attended Pacoima Jr. High School. (His third, posthumously issued album was Live at Pacoima Jr. High.) His first record, "Come On, Let's Go," nudged the charts early in 1958, and then in the fall of that year, the double-sided "Donna"/"La Bamba" rocketed to number two. Valens was on tour with Buddy Holly and The Big Bopper when their plane crashed outside of Clear Lake, Iowa, on February 3, 1959. All three were killed. In death, Ritchie remained a rock and roll hero and in 1987 his story was brought to the screen in *La Bamba*, a film shot in L.A. with music supplied by Los Lobos, four L.A. musicians who venerated him. Ritchie's mother lived to see that film, but died later in the year and was buried next to her son.

VALLEY MUSIC CENTER
(former location)
20600 Ventura
Woodland Hills

Rock bands played here in the sixties and seventies. There was the big concert on February 22, 1967, with The Doors, The Byrds and Buffalo Springfield. Subsequent shows featured Iron Butterfly, Canned Heat, Ike and Tina Turner, Badfinger, Billy Joel, Dick Dale and many others. But live music was falling on deaf ears at this end of the Valley by the late 1970's and the venue was converted to a Jehovah's Witnesses center in 1980.

VARIETY ARTS CENTER
Olympic & Figueroa
Downtown Los Angeles

Built in 1910, the building had a renaissance in the 1980s when Milt and Bill Larsen (the brothers who founded the Magic Castle magic club in Hollywood) turned it into a department store of music with four stories of entertainment—big bands on one floor, ragtime on another, etc.—accessible only by membership. (Occasionally rock bands were brought in for a general audience as when promoter Larry Vallon presented The Police here in 1980.) But by 1986 this idea had fizzled and booking was turned over to Masque/Club Lingerie booker Brendan Mullen, who booked in hot current acts like Jane's Addiction, The Red Hot Chili Peppers, The Replacements, Nick Cave, The Beastie Boys, Alex Chilton, Jonathan Richman, and nearly turned the place around. Unfortunately, location and indebtedness conspired to finally close the Center in 1988. It is currently undergoing renovation.

ART FEIN MOMENT #2:
VENTURA CLUB
2222 Ventura Blvd.
Sherman Oaks

This restaurant's live music policy has varied over the years but in 1974 when it featured supper-club acts I wandered in and spied an old black guy tooting a sax. Eager to get to a Mott The Hoople party or Jobriath's opening, I shrugged it off thinking "probably one of those 40s guys" and walked out on Louis Jordan.

VERBUM DEI HIGH SCHOOL
11100 South Central
Los Angeles

This Catholic high school (Verbum Dei means "Word of God" in Latin) deep in Watts has a heavily Louisiana-based constituency, and for the past fifteen years they've been running Louisiana-style "la las," featuring the best Zydeco acts in the country. In a down-home setting in the school gymnasium, they've presented Clifton Chenier, Queen Ida, Rockin' Dopsie, Wilfred Latour and John Delafosse. Visitors and parishioners come dressed up and ready to dance. The school serves soda and you can sample the gumbo and boudin sausage that's served out of the cloakroom. For fans of this kind of music, it's as close to Louisiana—or heaven—as you can get. Though they still talk about the time back

in 1979 that Mick Jagger showed up to see Clifton Chenier, this isn't a widely known venue—it's always been word-of mouth party for people who care.

VERTIGO CLUB

(former location)
4th & Boylston
Downtown Los Angeles
Even though disco had NOTH-
ING to do with rock & roll, we'll
include one reference. Originated in the late 1980s at
Myron's Ballroom in downtown
LA, Vertigo made international
headlines when Monaco's Prin-
cess Stephanie began turning
up. The club then moved to this
custom-built music center and ebbed and flowed for a while, then quit. Next, in 1992 or so, it
was called Glam Slam, licensing a name from Prince (he showed up here once), but it too soon
petered out.

GENE VINCENT GRAVE

Eternal Valley Memorial Park
Newhall

Gene Vincent's name and likeness are revered by rockers throughout the world. Based on his
leather motorcycle jacket and curly greased hair alone he could stand as an icon, but he had a
voice to match the image—"Be-Bop-A-Lula" stands as an anthem for rockers everywhere. Born
Vincent Eugene Craddock in Virginia, he came to Hollywood to try out for a Capitol Records
Elvis Presley "wannabe" contest and won hands down. "Be-Bop-A-Lula," recorded in Nashville, rocketed up the charts in mid-1956 and placed Vincent in the pantheon of rock idols of the
day. Unfortunately, he never had a follow-up hit as big, though he recorded many memorable
sides that are now treated like holy manna by rockers, especially in England and France. He
continued rocking into the sixties, despite the physical and psychological toll of having been in
a tragic 1960 car crash that killed his friend Eddie Cochran (See EDDIE COCHRAN). Vincent
limped before that crash from an injury sustained during the Korean War, the crash further
injuring his leg so that he lived the remainder of his life in nearly constant pain. By the mid-
1960s he was almost an Edith Piaf figure, a leather-clad rocker with a cane, posturing in ways

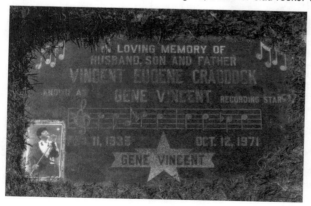

that wouldn't hurt him and
singing his heart out. Despite several comeback albums in the sixties,
Vincent's luck ran out on October 12, 1971, when he
died in Newhall of a bleed-
ing ulcer. (The much faded
photo on Vicent's headstone
was finally replaced but the
4th note of the "Be Bop A
Lula" excerpt on the headstone is still wrong.)

VIPER ROOM
8852 Sunset Blvd.
West Hollywood

Formerly The Central (See THE CENTRAL), The Viper Room was founded in 1993 by actor Johnny Depp and has proven to be a dependable showcase club for new and established bands — Aerosmith (investors) and many others (R.E.M., Porno For Pyros) have come here to play in a small club atmosphere. This club gained unfortunate notoriety in 1993 as the place where actor River Phoenix overdosed and died on the sidewalk in front of the club.

VITO'S PLACE
(former location)
303 N. Laurel
Hollywood

Diners at nearby Swingers restaurant may be hep but few know that within their view is the site of the studio and orgy-center run by the aged (in his 50s) hepcat sculptor Vito Paulekas in the 1960s. Vito taught sculpting classes here (in the basement below his wife Szou's custom-made clothing and thrift store) culling young girls, according to Pamela Des Barres' book *I'm With The Band*, until police harassment caused him to pack up and move north. He and his partner Carl Franzoni ran a free-form dance troupe which "freaked out" at rock shows by Love, The Seeds, The Byrds, The Mothers Of Invention and others. (Vito and Carl are cited on Freak Out.) He died October 25, 1992 in Santa Rosa, California (no obit in any L.A. paper) but he was rockin' to the very end, dancing at clubs in Northern California.

T-BONE WALKER GRAVE

Inglewood Park Cemetery
720 East Florence
Inglewood

Aaron "T-Bone" Walker (the nickname was a corruption of Thibeaux, his middle name) was a legendary blues-man whose guitar playing bridged blues and jazz. He was also the writer and first popularizer of "Stormy Monday," one of the most famous blues songs of all time. Born in Linden, Texas, Walker cut his teeth accompanying blues pioneers Ida Cox and Ma Rainey. Moving to California in 1934, he began his career in earnest in 1940 joining the bands of Fletcher Henderson and then Jack McVea, developing a singing style akin to shouting and a stinging guitar sound that made him a much-noticed presence on the blues scene. (His playing had an enormous influence on Chuck Berry—so, by extension, it influenced The Rolling Stones, The Beatles and everyone else that followed.) During his heyday on Capitol Records in the late forties, Walker's "Stormy Monday" brought him to the attention of the pop music world. He appeared on The Ed Sullivan Show and toured America extensively. He never had another hit as big as "Stormy Monday," but made excellent records for Imperial, Atlantic, Modern and other labels. During the early 1970s he played small clubs in L.A., often accompanied by future members of the blues-worshipping Blasters. His death of bronchial pneumonia in 1975 was a great loss to the music world.

WARNER BROS. RECORDS

3300 Warner Boulevard
Burbank

The giant record company (which is only a branch of mega-giant Warner Communications) operates from this tasteful wood-forest building in Burbank's entertainment district. Currently on the roster are Alanis Morissette, Madonna, R.E.M., Eric Clapton and literally a hundred others. (Don't show up outside with your guitar and your glossies, send a tape.)

WARNER BROS. STUDIOS

Barham & Franklin
Burbank

If the entrance looks familiar, it's because you saw it in the finale of *Blazing Saddles*—but that's not what we're concerned with after all this is a music book—somewhere on this lot, the picture was taken for the cover of the Pink Floyd album *Wish You Were Here*.

JOHNNY "GUITAR" WATSON CRYPT

Forest Lawn
Glendale

The man who virtually de-
fined rock & roll guitar-playing lived most of his life in
the L.A. area, arriving from
Texas in 1950. At first he
waxed aggressive, growling
blues for many labels, including Combo, Federal, and LA-
based RPM. (Those RPM

sides are so blistering they may detonate your CD player. Frank Zappa said the one record he
would take to a desert island was Watson's "Three Hours Past Midnight.") In the early 60s he
had hits with King Records, in the late 60s he performed and recorded with Larry Williams and
in 1977 he scored a funk hit, "A Real Mother For Ya." His career cooled in the 80s, but rose
back up in the 90s with his re-discovery by a new wave of music fans. He died suddenly onstage
in 1996 during a concert tour of Japan.

WENZEL'S MUSIC TOWN

13117 Lakewood
Downey

Tom and Maxine Wenzel run a nice oldies
record store with a heavy history. The
"collector's room" used to be a recording
studio where "Pipeline" by the Chantays
and "Boss" by The Rumblers were recorded in the early 1960's and released on
(Tom's father) Bill Wenzel's Downey label.
Legend has it that "Cinnamon Cinder" by
the Pastel Six was recorded here too, but
actually it was its flip side, "Bandido," according to industry veteran Russ Regan,
who wrote the song. (Regan, who worked
closely with many surf groups in the early
1960s, actually gave The Beach Boys, frequent Wenzel's customers, their name and
later founded Uni Records.) The Beach
Boys recorded "Wipe Out" here in 1962.
Producer Dale Smallin (he cackles at the
start of "Wipe Out") had them do a hand-
ful of surf instrumentals for a local film
called *One Man's Challenge.*

THE WHISKY-A-GO-GO
8901 Sunset Blvd.
West Hollywood

Now primarily used by hard rock bands, this was the club in the sixties and seventies. Who played here? Where do you start? The Kinks, Led Zeppelin, The Who, Cream, The Doors, Otis Redding (whose LP *Live at the Whisky* was recorded here in 1967) Jimi Hendrix, The Byrds, Talking Heads, AC/DC—the list would fill this book. The Whisky-A-Go-Go opened in 1964 on the site of an old bank building that had been remodeled into a short-lived club called The Party. Though billed as a "discotheque"—meaning no bands, just records—The Whisky opened with a live band led by Johnny Rivers and a short-skirted deejay spinning records between sets from a suspended cage at the right of the stage. When the girl danced during Rivers' set, the audience thought it was part of the act and the concept of "go-go" girls was born. Rivers rode The Whisky-born "go-go" craze to national fame with records recorded (partly) *Live at the Whisky.* The Miracles recorded "Going to a Go-Go" in 1966 (it was covered in 1982 by The Rolling Stones) and Whisky-A-Go-Go franchises sprung up all over America. In 1966 the Whisky was one of the centers of the Sunset Strip riots. It was hassled repeatedly by the city, which once ordered the club to change its name, claiming "Whisky" was a bad influence (does anyone remember when it was The Whisk?). The Doors, who played every club in town including The London Fog next door, settled in for a long run here and subsequently rode to worldwide fame. The rockin' didn't stop till the late seventies, when live music venues fell on hard times. The Whisky closed in 1982 and reopened as a "four-wall" (promoters renting it) in 1986. Today the Whisky is at the eastern end of an active hard rock "strip" not dissimilar to that of the halcyon days of the sixties. The club was originally painted red, then changed over the years (in early 1990 it was repainted red and its old striped awnings restored for the movie The Doors.

CLARENCE WHITE GRAVE
Joshua Memorial Park
Lancaster

Clarence White's country guitar playing had a tremendous impact in the late sixties and early seventies. From his first work with his brothers Roland and Eric in the Kentucky Colonels to session work with Linda Ronstadt, Joe Cocker, Randy Newman, Arlo Guthrie and others, through his association with The Byrds from 1968 to 1973, he turned a lot of people on to country music. He died tragically in 1973, run down by a drunk driver while loading instruments into a car outside the Jack O' Diamonds club (since burned down) in Palmdale, California. Shortly after White's death, his wife and two of his children were killed in a car crash. They are buried near him in this cemetery.

WILD THING
(former location)
Cahuenga south of Yucca
Hollywood

The Wild Thing was a rock and roll nightclub of the mid-1960s that featured at least one historically significant act. Johnny Legend, whose band played there, swears he remembers them advertising the first (and only?) performance of Jerry "Leave It to Beaver" Mathers' rock band: Beaver and The Trappers. (Mathers made two rock singles: the adenoidal "Wind Up Toy," by Jerry Mathers on Atlantic, and the pretty decent "Happiness is Havin'" by Beaver and The Trappers on White Cliff.) Frank Zappa's map cites this place as a venue for the West Coast Pop Art Experimental Band and The Knack (who soon disappeared, only to have their name revived by the "My Sharona" guys in 1979 — and both were on Capitol!).

WILL ROGERS MEMORIAL PARK
Sunset & Canon
Beverly Hills

Rodeo philosopher Will Rogers said he'd never met a man he didn't like, often while twirling a coiled rope. Pop singer George Michaels was of much the same mind (if charges against him are true) when he was arrested in this bathroom just before 5 p.m on 4/8/98; the arresting officer says Michaels, also, was twirling something.

BRIAN WILSON FORMER RESIDENCE

10452 Bellagio Road
Beverly Hills
(Do Not Disturb Occupants)

While living here and record-ing in his home studio, Brian Wilson created the Beach Boys' *Smiley Smile* album. On the *Friends* album, the song "Busy Doin' Nothing" hazily describes the route to this house, not unlike Billy Strayhorne's directions to Duke Ellington's in "Take the 'A' Train." (Around 1968 you wouldn't have needed directions to this house: it stood out like a beacon after Wilson painted it purple, enraging neighbors but not seriously affecting real estate values.) Actually, most of the albums *Smiley Smile, Wild Honey, Friends, 20/20, Sunflower, Surf's Up,* and *Carl & The Passions: So Tough* were recorded in his home studio here. However, this is not where Wilson constructed a sandbox to surround his piano (to get a "beach" feeling) and erected a circus tent. That was another house, on Laurel Way.

DENNIS WILSON DEATH SITE

13929 Bellagio Way,
Basin C-1100
Marina Del Rey

Dennis Wilson was the drummer, sex symbol and only real surfer of The Beach Boys. During the 1970s his talent as pro-ducer and songwriter came to the forefront both on Beach Boys records and on his solo album *Pacific Ocean Blue* (1977). Dennis was the most individualistic Beach Boy. In 1968 he became in-volved with Charles Manson (Manson's song "Cease to Exist" was altered to "Never Learn Not to Love" and released as a Beach Boys B-side.) In 1971, he appeared in the film *Two Lane Blacktop* with James Taylor. By the late 1970s Dennis' prodigious drug and alcohol intake began to take its toll. His on-stage antics became painful to see (at Beach Boys concerts in the early 1980s he was trotted out not unlike the palsied Joe Cocker to sing Cocker's "You Are So Beautiful.") Wilson was visiting a friend in the Marina the night of December 28, 1983 when he drowned while diving for 'souveniers' thrown by friends. His ashes were scattered at sea at the behest of his widow, Shawn Love Wilson (the alleged illegitimate daughter of his cousin and fellow Beach Boy, Mike Love).

X FORMER RESIDENCE
1118 North Genesee
West Hollywood
(Do Not Disturb Occupants)

When X hit the music scene in 1978, it hit hard, with the biting lyrical imagery of lead singers John Doe and Exene Cervenka, D.J. Bonebrake's powerful drumming, and Billy Zoom's stunning rockabilly guitar. It was a group that dominated L.A.'s new music scene from their inception to their more or less dissolution in 1988. John and Exene lived in this house in the early days. Much of the X footage in *The Decline of Western Civilization*, the Penelope Spheeris film that documented the nascent punk movement, was shot here as were the back cover photos on X's *Wild Gift* album.

YOU'VE GOT BAD TASTE
3816 Sunset Blvd.
Silverlake

As a new-and-used gift shop, this place fits well in the worn and comfortable Silverlake District, but what makes it stand out is a Punk-Rock Museum installed by the store's owners, John Roeker and Exene Cervenka (formerly of the band X).

FRANK ZAPPA
FORMER RESIDENCE #1
(now torn down)
NW corner of Laurel Canyon & Lookout Mountain
Laurel Canyon

Frank Zappa lived here in a log cabin formerly owned by cowboy actor Tom Mix, from 1966 to 1968, when he left because too many weirdos were dropping in (not including John Mayall, who lived here with Zappa when he first came to the U.S.) Eric Burdon rented it after that. It burned down around 1980. Zappa's influence both personal and musical cannot be overstated. His concerts with his band The Mothers of Invention, originally billed as "freak-outs," set the stage for the performance art of the future and spread a kind of liberating madness around L.A.

that was far more insidious than what the hippies were doing in San Francisco. Yet Zappa was a highly disciplined band leader and composer, a non-drug user who never hesitated to mock the sacred icons and gurus of hippie culture along with the police, the government, even war toy manufacturers. To Zappa, California was full of conformist "Plastic People," young and old. The Mothers of Invention audaciously debuted with a double album which included a track about the Watts riots, "Trouble Coming Every Day," that has never been topped for telling it like it is about Los Angeles. Zappa was later championed by L.A. Philharmonic conductor Zubin Mehta, who premiered one of Zappa's orchestral works at UCLA's Pauley Pavilion. (The performance included not only adventurous music, but various Mothers sticking stuffed giraffes up the skirts of female cellists.) Because Zappa was a consummate businessman not averse to going to court to protect himself, he personally owns every significant shred of tape he ever recorded, and carefully released hours of historical performance on his Barking Pumpkin label. He was an outspoken advocate of free speech, was working on Eastern European trade issues and became a friend of Czechoslovakian President Vaclav Havel. Sadly, Frank Zappa died in 1993.

FRANK ZAPPA
FORMER RESIDENCE #2
1819 Bellevue
Los Angeles
While the Laurel Canyon residence is Frank's most famous, it was here, in 1965, that he wrote the bulk of the Mothers Of Invention's *Freak Out* album when not working (and probably while working) as a clerk at Wallich's Music City record store in Hollywood.

ZAPPA RECORDS

11696 Ventura Blvd.

Studio City

After fighting in court against every major label he was on, Frank Zappa launched his own label, Zappa Records in the late 1970s. The first two releases on this imprint, *Sheik Yerbouti* and *Joe's Garage* were among his most successful. That label gave way to the Barking Pumpkin moniker in the early 1980s, which had the hit "Valley Girl." Towards the end of his life Zappa made a lucrative deal with Ryko Records to release his back catalog, while new Zappa product continues to be issued from this location.

ZERO ZERO CLUB

(former location)

1957 Cahuenga

Hollywood

During the big LA-music time of 1980-1985, this was an after-hours club known for its inverse exclusiveness—you had to be a musician or a loyal follower to get in. (The 'reversal' is that these are the kind of people most decent places want to keep out!) Dave Alvin remembers the night everyone was asked by the police to get on the floor and be frisked after neighbors complained of noise disturbance. Featured a lot in the LA Weekly.

ACKNOWLEDGMENTS

So many people helped in the preparation of this book that it would be impossible to single anyone out. Thanks to one and all.

Mary Katherine Aldin, David Alexander, Dave Alvin, Alison Anders, Gayle Anderson, Eddie Angel, James Austin, Cary Baker, Michael Barackman, Dan Barrett, George Barris, J.R. Bell, Kent Benjamin, Bill Bentley, Bill Berry, Jim Bickhart, Bob Biggs, Greg Biggs, Rodney Bingenheimer, Dick Blackburn, Joe Blackstock, Hal Blaine, Joseph Blockstock, Ruben Blue, Paul Body, Mars Bonfire, Donna Boni, Sonny Bono, Dan Bourgouise, Bruce Bromberg, Harold Bronson, Kip Brown, Leonard Brown, Tom Brown, Denny Bruce, Carol Bua, Clair Brush, Paul Buff, Bug Music, Pat Burnette, Cliff Burnstein, Hamilton Camp, Ray Campi, Kim Canoe, Jerry Capehart, John Carter, Ben Chase-Harper, Roger Christian, Billyl Cioffi, Susan Clary, Jamie Cohen, Bud Cort, Denise Cox, Sue Crawford, Marshall Crenshaw, Richard Cromelin, Davenport, Gerard Bart David, Cameron Davis, Saul Davis, Jim Dawson, Mark Deaver, John Delgatto, Darryl DeLoach, Lisa Demberg, Pamela Des Barres, Dave DiMartino, Derek Dickerson, Henry Diltz, Dobbs, John Doe, Corb Donohue, Bruce Duff, Bill Earl, Ken Ehrlich, John Einarson, James Ellroy, Bob Emmer, Laura Engel, Kristine Estlund, Todd Everett, Len Fagan, Steve Farber, Doug Fieger, Harvey Sid Fisher, Kurt Fisher, Ben Fong-Torres, Richard Foos, Tina Forde, Kim Fowley, Pete Frame, Carl Franzoni, Donna Freberg, Stan Freberg, Barry Friedman, Dianne Gardiner, Kim Gardner, Janis Garza, Pleasant Gehman, Melinda Sue Gordon, Wavy Gravy, Paul Greenstein, Paul Grein, Sid Griffin, Vicky Hamilton, Paul Hampton, Jack Hanna, Barry Hansen, Steve Harvey, Skip Heller, Bob Hilburn, Chris Hillman, Connie Hillman, Richard Hite, Steve Hochman, Jerry Hopkins, Walter Hurst, Danny Hutton, Elliot Ingber, Ken Jacobs, Billy James, John Johnson, Bruce Johnston, Fredda Joiner, Lee Joseph, Yorma Kahana, Phil Kaufman, Bob Keene, Elliot Kendall, Kevin Kennedy, Tom Kenny, Iris Keitel, King Cotton, Lisa Kirk, Terry Kirkman, Allen Klein, Jody Klein, Al Kooper, Paul Krassner, Art Laboe, Kenny Laguna, Alan Larman, Grelun Landon, Tito Larriva, Byron Laursen, Larry Lazar, David Leaf, Malcom Leo, Robert Leslie, Corey Leviton, Mark Leviton, Bill Liebowitz, Limey Dave, Lisa Lindstrom, Rich Linnell, Greg Loescher, Victoria Looseleaf, Phil MacConnell, Ron & Russell Mael, Toby Mamis, Anna Martinez-Holler, Jimmy Maslon, Phillipe Manoevre, Rip Masters, John Mayall, Filthy McNasty, Stephen McParland, Bill Medley, Bob Merlis, Betty Miller, Don Misraje, Jim Monsour, Paul Moratta, Darryl Morden, Chris Morris, Keith Morris, Bill Morrison, Brendan Mullen, Music Connection Magazine, Sandy Nelson, Tim Nolan, Michael Ochs, Andrew Oldham, Jimmy O'Neill, Johnny Otis, Andy Paley, Van Dyke Parks, Clay Pasternak, Jennifer Pelphrey, Hank Penny, Bill Peterson, Debbie Peterson, Jim Pewter, Phast Phreddie, Lori E. Pike, Paul Politti, Steve Pond, Domenic Priore, Steve Propes, Aron Rapaport, Dr. Don Reed, Russ Regan, Jeff Ressner, Gail Roberts, Heidi Robinson, Steve Roeser, Henry Rollins, Cesar Rosas, Sandra Rosas, Beverly Rupe, Simon Rutberg, Rob Santos, Chris Sayadian, Kathe Schreyer, Hugh Scott, Gene Sculatti, Joel Selvin, Greg Shaw, Suzy Shaw, Sharon Sheeley, Bobby Sheen, Suzanne Sherwin, John Silva, Neil Skok, Brian Slagel, Phillip Sloan, Don Snowden, David Somerville, The Sprague Bros, Linda Stevens, Gary Stewart, Jeff Stolper, Cliffie Stone, Ron Stone, Dave Stuckey, Danny Sugerman, John Sutherland, Billy Swan, Russ Tamblyn, Malcom Tent, The Topanga Messenger, Dean Torrence, Pam Turbov, Ike Turner, Jeanette Turner, Dwight Twilley, Gary Usher, Larry Vallon, Johnny Vargas, Nik Venet, Billy Vera, Russ Wapensky, Ed Ward, Guy Webster, Frank Weimann, Ron Weiser, Chuck E. Weiss, Geroge Wendt, Ian Whitcomb, Alan White, Mindi White, Timothy White, Dootsie Williams, Jerry "Swamp Dogg" Williams, Paul Williams, Mike Willard, Erin Yasgar, Dwight Yoakam

Other books from 2.13.61:

HENRY ROLLINS / The First Five
HENRY ROLLINS / Black Coffee Blues
HENRY ROLLINS / See A Grown Man Cry — Now Watch Him Die
HENRY ROLLINS / Get In The Van
HENRY ROLLINS / Eye Scream
HENRY ROLLINS / Do I Come Here Often?
JOE COLE / Planet Joe
DON BAJEMA / Reach
DON BAJEMA / Boy In The Air
BILL SHIELDS / Human Shrapnel
BILL SHIELDS / The Southeast Asian Book Of The Dead
BILL SHIELDS / Lifetaker
BILL SHIELDS / Rosey the Baby Killer and Other Stories
EXENE CERVENKA / Virtual Unreality
EXENE CERVENKA & KEN JARECKE / Just Another War
ELLYN MAYBE / The Cowardice of Amnesia
IAN SHOALES / Not Wet Yet
IGGY POP / I Need More
TRICIA WARDEN / Brainlift
TRICIA WARDEN / Attack God Inside
MICHAEL GIRA / The Consumer
ROB OVERTON / Letters To Rollins
NICK CAVE / King Ink
NICK CAVE / King Ink II
NICK CAVE & THE BAD SEEDS / Fish In A Barrel
ALAN VEGA / Cripple Nation
ROSS HALFIN / Fragile: Human Organs
ROSS HALFIN / Metallica: The Photographs of Ross Halfin
STEPHANIE CHERNIKOWSKI / Dream Baby Dream
THE PHOTOGRAPHER'S LED ZEPPELIN
ROKY ERICKSON / Openers II
JOE CARDUCCI / Rock & the Pop Narcotic
NICK ZEDD / Totem Of The Depraved
HENRY MILLER / Dear Dear Brenda